COLUMBIA

1000

WORDS YOU

MUST KNOW

for IELTS™

BOOK TWO WITH ANSWERS

Richard Lee, Ph.D.

COLUMBIA PRESS

All inquiries should be addressed to:

Columbia Press International

803-470 Granville Street

Vancouver, BC V6C 1V5

Email: richardleephd@hotmail.com

ISBN-13： 978-1-927647-15-8

To Nancy, Philip, and Christina

CONTENTS

TO THE STUDENT...ix

Unit 1...12
    jocund, refund, rotund, moribund, rubicund
    laborious, pernicious, avaricious, inauspicious, prejudicious

Unit 2...16
    lacerate, advocate, consolidate, intimidate, precipitate
    lambent, nascent, imminent, penitent, pertinent

Unit 3...20
    lampoon, lagoon, monsoon, platoon, tycoon
    largess, digress, duress, obsess, transgress

Unit 4...24
    legion, fusion, precision, profusion, introversion
    lucrative, abortive, conducive, cumulative, diminutive

Unit 5...28
    lull, dull, gull, null, skull
    lurid, rid, acrid, forbid, rigid

Unit 6...32
    malediction, friction, addiction, conviction, jurisdiction
    malign, align, assign, consign, resign

Unit 7...36
    materiality, brutality, fatality, formality, morality
    mercenary, adversary, centenary, mortuary, planetary

Unit 8..40
  mitigate, innate, emulate, oscillate, propagate
  mollify, certify, ossify, vilify, rectify

Unit 9..44
  mordant, penchant, petulant, rampant, recalcitrant
  morose, compose, dispose, foreclose, verbose

Unit 10..48
  mundane, humane, insane, profane, hurricane
  munificent, consent, extent, aliment, regiment

Unit 11..52
  nefarious, precarious, vicarious, multifarious, temerarious
  nemesis, thesis, mimesis, exegesis, telekinesis

Unit 12..56
  neophyte, byte, acolyte, proselyte, troglodyte
  neoteric, generic, numeric, atmospheric, esoteric

Unit 13..60
  nettle, fettle, mettle, settle, unsettle
  niggard, bard, discard, retard, safeguard

Unit 14..64
  noxious, precious, nutritious, obnoxious, ostentatious
  nugatory, mandatory, purgatory, signatory, defamatory

Unit 15..68
  obeisance, askance, enhance, nuance, renaissance
  obfuscate, castigate, deprecate, articulate, inveterate

Unit 16..72
  objurgate, enunciate, exculpate, extrapolate, facilitate
  obtrude, delude, aptitude, lassitude, rectitude

Unit 17..76
  odious, factious, facetious, fortuitous, disputatious
  oligarchy, anarchy, monarchy, hierarchy, patriarchy

Unit 18..80
  opalescent, ferment, fervent, putrescent, adolescent
  opprobrious, captious, horrendous, lecherous, mellifluous

Unit 19..84
  originate, inculcate, instigate, litigate, immaculate
  ozone, clone, condone, cyclone, silicone

Unit 20..88
  palpable, viable, tractable, immutable, irreparable
  paradox, jukebox, smallpox, equinox, orthodox

Unit 21..92
parity, brevity, alacrity, depravity, disparity
parsimonious, arduous, amorphous, ambiguous, anonymous

Unit 22..96
paucity, probity, frugality, humility, impunity
penury, fury, jury, , mercury, perjury

Unit 23..100
perdition, aspersion, abnegation, adulation, implication
peremptory, allegory, dilatory, inventory, perfunctory

Unit 24..104
perfidious, tenuous, momentous, ominous, vociferous
peruse, fuse, muse, abuse, interfuse

Unit25..108
pervasive, abrasive, dissuasive, evasive, persuasive
petition, rendition, acquisition, coalition, intuition

Unit 26..112
polemic, endemic, systemic, epidemic, epistemic
portend, blend, amend, apprehend, reprehend

Unit 27..116
precept, concept, incept, inept, intercept
precocious, spacious, specious, atrocious, ferocious

Unit 28..120
preponderate, prate, profligate, elaborate, repudiate
prerogative, correlative, derivative, figurative, preservative

Unit 29..124
prognosis, hypnosis, diagnosis, scoliosis, tuberculosis
prolific, horrific, specific, terrific, colorific

Unit 30..128
prognosticate, implicate, reiterate, relegate, eradicate
propitiate, deviate, initiate, mediate, differentiate

Unit 31..132
protocol, menthol, alcohol, parasol, cholesterol
provident, diffident, evident, incident, coincident

Unit 32..136
puerile, agile, docile, exile, futile
purloin, adjoin, conjoin, disjoin, rejoin

Unit 33..140
purview, preview, review, worldview, interview
putrefy, classify, justify, qualify, sanctify

Unit 34..144

quagmire, acquire, aspire, conspire, respire
quarantine, chlorine, cuisine, marine, pristine

Unit 35..148
    quintessence, sequence, diligence, indulgence, intelligence
    quizzical, radical, illogical, sabbatical, chronological

Answer Key...152

Word Index...161

Acknowledgments...175

About the Author..177

TO THE STUDENT

The shortest and best way of learning a language is to know the roots of it, that is, those original primitive words from which other words are formed.

-- Lord Chesterfield

Columbia 1000 Words You Must Know for IELTS presents 1000 most frequently tested words for IELTS. You will find 100 vocabulary-building lessons in Books 1 – 3. Each lesson contains 10 new words and they are first presented to you with **Memory Tips**; next, **New Words** are listed in rhyming memory groups and followed by **Sample Sentences**; the last part of the lesson are **Sentence Completion** and **Definition Matching** practice tests with answers. One of the most outstanding features of this book is that each new word is repeated at least five times in a lesson so that you will have a much better chance to memorize it more easily.

Columbia 1000 Words You Must Know for IELTS is designed to help you master all the absolutely essential IELTS words using our most effective memory method: **A Roots and Rhyming Memory Approach**. Let's take the word "**aberration**" for example and see how this exciting new memory method can help you find the shortest and best way to memorize new words and build a large vocabulary:

1. **MEMORY TIPS:** Memorizing words with the help of Roots, Prefixes, and Suffixes.

    ion   condition or action; as ***aberration***, *ration, inflation, temptation, abbreviation*

2. **NEW WORDS:** New Words are arranged in rhyming groups for easy memory.

aberration	*ration*	*inflation*	*temptation*	*abbreviation*

ABERRATION [ˌæbəˈreɪʃ(ə)n] *n.* departure from what is right or true   **rhyming sound –ation**

3. **SAMPLE SENTENCES**: Sample Sentences are given to help you memorize words in context.

   *This complexity is not an **aberration** or something to be wished away, it is the new reality.*

4. **SENTENCE COMPLETION**: Sentence Completion is designed to help you memorize words through tests.

   *The patient's only _____ was a temporary lapse of memory. **(aberration)***

5. **DEFINITION MATCHING**: Definition Matching is designed to help you memorize words through repetition.

   *departure from what is right or true _____ **(aberration)***

In this example, the repeated appearance of the word "**aberration**" in the lesson makes it easy for you to memorize. Therefore you can see that only by repeated practice or reinforcement of a new word under different circumstances can you really memorize it so unconsciously that you will never forget. Human memory, like the unconscious, is structured like a language. Once you have memorized a new word, it will stay in your unconscious and become part of yourself. Whenever you need it, it will come to you automatically just like the flowers coming in the spring: it is natural!

Columbia 1000 Words You Must Know for IELTS is both a self-help book and a textbook for classroom use. It is the only vocabulary book you will ever need to master the most often tested words on the IELTS. If you can spend about 25 minutes a day with this book, you will definitely help yourself expand your vocabulary, build up your word power, and raise your score on the IELTS.

Richard Lee, Ph.D.

Beautiful Vancouver

UNIT 1

MEMORY TIPS:

Word building with Roots, Prefixes, and Suffixes:

---

in	not; as *inauspicious*
ious	characterized by; as *laborious, pernicious, avaricious, inauspicious*
pre	before; as *prejudicious*
re	back, again; as *refund*

NEW WORDS

jocund	refund	rotund	moribund	rubicund
laborious	pernicious	avaricious	inauspicious	prejudicious

1. JOCUND   ['dʒɑkənd] *adj.* happy and cheerful   **rhyming sound –und**

Mary could not but be gay in such a **jocund** company on campus.

Word Families: **jocundity** *n.*; **jocundly** *adv.*

2. refund   ['ri,fʌnd] *v.* to pay back; *n.* return of money

We offer guaranteed **refund** of any defective goods in our store.

Word Families: **refundable** *adj.*

3. rotund   [roʊ'tʌnd] *adj.* round and fat; having a full and rich sound

He was a large **rotund** man with a very jovial nature and a compassionate disposition.

4. moribund ['mɔrə,bʌnd] *adj.* no longer effective and not likely to continue for much longer

We believe that imperialism is monopolistic, parasitic and **moribund** capitalism.

5. rubicund ['rubɪkənd] *adj.* having a red face

The woman's **rubicund** face expressed consternation and fatigue.

6. LABORIOUS [lə'bɔriəs] *adj* .involving great prolonged effort   **rhyming sound -ious**

The process was **laborious**, but I had no reason to complain of the way

it miraculously worked.

7. pernicious [pər'nɪʃəs] *adj.* very dangerous or harmful, especially to one's character

We did what we could, but her mother's influence on her was **pernicious**.

Word Families: **perniciousness** *n.;* **perniciously** *adv.*

8. avaricious [,ævə'rɪʃəs] *adj.* showing an unreasonable desire to obtain and keep money

Mary sacrificed her career so that her **avaricious** husband could succeed.

Word Families: **avariciousness** *n.;* **avarice** *n.;* **avariciously** *adv.*

9. inauspicious [,ɪnɔ'spɪʃəs] *adj.* unlucky, likely to have an unfavorable outcome

For the Americans, number 13 is considered as an **inauspicious** number.

Word Families: **inauspiciousness** *n.;* **inauspiciously** *adv.*

10. prejudicious [,prɛdʒə'dɪʃəs] *adj.* damaging to career and reputation

The reporter's coverage was **prejudicious** to the mayor's campaign.

SENTENCE COMPLETION

Choose one of the new words to complete each sentence below. Make changes if necessary.

jocund	refund	rotund	moribund	rubicund
laborious	pernicious	avaricious	inauspicious	prejudicious

1. People tend to believe that it is _____ to walk under a ladder.

2. Our boss is a pleasant _____ little man; he always looks very well-fed.

3. We should not despise plain features, nor a _____ yet honest occupation.

4. I could not but be gay in such a _____ company.

5. The little girl watched the color drain from her father's _____ face.

6. Smoking is absolutely _____ to our health.

7. The US dollar, a once proud and honest currency, is _____, like the nation it represents.

8. Almost all stores will _____ your money if you're not happy with your purchase.

9. The _____ report about the Governor's affairs contributed to his downfall.

10. This businessman is so _____ that everybody calls him a blood sucker.

DEFINITION MATCHING

Choose one of the new words to match each definition below

jocund	refund	rotund	moribund	rubicund
laborious	pernicious	avaricious	inauspicious	prejudicious

11. round and fat _____

12. involving great prolonged effort _____

13. having a red face _____

14. damaging to career and reputation _____

15. to pay back _____

16. very dangerous or harmful _____

17. unreasonably desiring to obtain and keep money_____

18. no longer effective and not likely to continue _____

19. unlucky _____

20. happy and gay _____

WRITING SENTENCES

Use each new word in the box to write an original sentence.

jocund	refund	rotund	moribund	rubicund
laborious	pernicious	avaricious	inauspicious	prejudicious

21._____

22._____

23._____

24._____

25._____

26._____

27._____

28._____

29._____

30._____

UNIT 2

MEMORY TIPS:

Word building with Roots, Prefixes, and Suffixes:

---

ate	one who; as *lacerate, advocate, consolidate, intimidate, precipitate*
im, in	into, in, on; as *imminent, intimidate*
nasc	be from, to spring forth; as *nascent*
pre	before; as *precipitate*

NEW WORDS

lacerate	advocate	consolidate	intimidate	precipitate
lambent	nascent	imminent	penitent	pertinent

1. LACERATE   ['læsə,reɪt] *v.* to make a deep cut in someone's flesh   **rhyming sound –ate**

The man kept drifting about to find Judy and **lacerate** her with the performance.

Word Families: **laceration** *n.*

2. advocate   ['ædvəkət] *v.* to publicly support a policy or a way of doing things; n. a lawyer; someone who publicly supports someone or something

Michael Freeman is a strong **advocate** of prison freedom.

Word Families: **advocation** *n.*

3. consolidate [kən'sɑlɪ,deɪt] *v.* to make or become stronger or more stable

With the release of his new movie he has **consolidated** his **position** as the country's leading director.
Word Families: **consolidation** *n.;* **consolidator** *n.*

4. intimidate [ɪn'tɪmɪ,deɪt] *v.* to deliberately make someone feel frightened

His vicious attempts to **intimidate** people into voting for the governing party did not work.

Word Families: **intimidation** *n.;* **intimidator** *n.;* **intimidating** *adj.*

5. precipitate [prɪ'sɪpɪ,tet] *v.* to cause to happen suddenly; *adj.* done rashly or hastily

Most of our financial problems have been caused by **precipitate** policy making in the past.

Word Families: **precipitable** *adj.*

6. LAMBENT ['læmbənt] *adj.* softly gleaming or glowing   **rhyming sound -ent**

There was a continual play of **lambent** fire about her charming eyes.

Word Families: **lambency** *n.;* **lambently** *adv.*

7. nascent ['næs(ə)nt] *adj.* beginning or formed recently

The fund management industry in the country is still at a **nascent** stage.

8. imminent ['ɪmɪnənt] *adj.* likely or certain to happen very soon

People feel that a disaster is **imminent**, as if a catastrophe is about to come.

Word Families: **imminence** *n.;* **imminently** *adv.*

9. penitent ['penɪtənt] *adj.* feeling sorry for having done wrong

He has grown neither humble nor **penitent** by what has passed.

Word Families: **penitence** *n.;* **penitently** *adv.*

10. pertinent ['pɜrt(ə)nənt] *adj.* relevant to something

We shall now consider **pertinent** information on recent developments in cardiac electrophysiology.

Word Families: **pertinence** *n.;* **pertinently** *adv.*

SENTENCE COMPLETION

Choose one of the new words to complete each sentence below. Make changes if necessary.

lacerate	advocate	consolidate	intimidate	precipitate
lambent	nascent	imminent	penitent	pertinent

1. Johnson is a conservative who _____ less government control on business.

2. The _____ glow of fireflies made us feel like we were in a wonderland.

3. She was suffering from a badly _____ hand.

4. It looks like the country is in _____ danger of war.

5. We should never make _____ decision in business.

6. China is a _____ economic superpower.

7. The Senate and House hearing rooms are designed to _____ the witness.

8. She has asked some _____ questions about the project.

9. Michael Jones _____ his lead in the National League when he won the latest round.

10. The _____ girl turned her back on the unhappy past and began a new life.

DEFINITION MATCHING

Choose one of the new words to match each definition below.

lacerate	advocate	consolidate	intimidate	precipitate
lambent	nascent	imminent	penitent	pertinent

11. to cause to happen suddenly _____

12. relevant to something _____

13. to make or become stronger or more stable _____

14. feeling sorry for having done wrong _____

15. to deliberately make someone feel frightened _____

16. to make a deep cut in someone's flesh _____

17. likely or certain to happen very soon _____

18. softly gleaming or glowing _____

19. beginning or formed recently _____

20. to publicly support a policy or action _____

WRITING SENTENCES

Use each new word in the box to write an original sentence.

lacerate	advocate	consolidate	intimidate	precipitate
lambent	nascent	imminent	penitent	pertinent

21. _____

22. _____

23. _____

24. _____

25. _____

26. _____

27. _____

28. _____

29. _____

30. _____

UNIT 3

MEMORY TIPS:

Word building with Roots, Prefixes, and Suffixes:

---

di	apart, not; as *digress*
ob	against; as *obsess*
trans	across, beyond, change; as *transgress*

NEW WORDS

lampoon	lagoon	monsoon	platoon	tycoon
largess	digress	duress	obsess	transgress

1. LAMPOON [læmˈpun] *v.* to satirize or ridicule; *n.* humorous satire ridiculing someone
rhyming sound –oon

He denied praising the North Korean government and said that his intention was to **lampoon** the North Korean regime.

Word Families: **lampooner** *n.;* **lampoonist** *n.*

2. lagoon [ləˈgun] *n.* a shallow lake or channel

The **lagoon** was pullulated with dead fish.

3. monsoon [mɑnˈsun] *n.* seasonal wind of SE Asia; rainy season accompanying

seasonal wind

The south-west **monsoon** sets in during April.

Word Families: **monsoonal** *adj.*

4. platoon   [pləˈtun] *n.* a small group of soldiers that a lieutenant is in charge of

Our **platoon** was probing the enemy from an advanced position.

5. tycoon   [taɪˈkuːn] *n.* a rich and powerful person

Russian **tycoon** Boris Berezovsky loses his court battle against Roman Abramovich.

6. LARGESS   [lɑrˈʒɛs] *n.* a generous giving, especially of money   **rhyming sound -ess**

In 2006, the donation had a value of $30 billion, making it the biggest philanthropic **largess** in history.

7. digress   [daɪˈgres] *v.* to depart from the main subject in speech and writing

She **digressed** from her prepared speech to pay tribute to the President.

Word Families: **digression** *n.;* **digressive** *adj.;* **digressively** *adv.*

8. duress   [dʊˈres] *n.* compulsion by use of force or threats

She acknowledged that she had signed the agreement under **duress**.

9. obsess   [əbˈses] *v.* to worry about something all the time

People who **obsess** about clothes also **obsess** about shoes, particularly men.

Word Families: **obsession** *n;* **obsessive** *adj.;* **obsessively** *adv.*

10. transgress   [trænzˈgres] *v.* to break (a moral law, custom or religion)

No one is permitted to have privileges to **transgress** the law.

Word Families: **transgression** *n.;* **transgressor** *n.*

SENTENCE COMPLETION

Choose one of the new words to complete each sentence below. Make changes if necessary.

lampoon	lagoon	monsoon	platoon	tycoon
largess	digress	duress	obsess	transgress

1. You should be generous and give _____ to everyone when you are rich.

2. His inexperience made him easy to _____.

3. We shall not _____ into the history of mechanics.

4. Those who acted under _____ shall go unpunished.

5. The _____ will run to the end of next month.

6. A girdle of islands enclosed the _____.

7. Equity investors should not _____ over economic growth.

8. His _____ made its way to the pre-arranged rendezvous in the desert.

9. A leading philanthropist and cosmetics _____ plans to donate 78 Cubist works to the New York Metropolitan Museum of Art.

10. We should not _____ the commandment of the Lord.

DEFINITION MATCHING

Choose one of the new words to match each definition below.

lampoon	lagoon	monsoon	platoon	tycoon
largess	digress	duress	obsess	transgress

11. to depart from the main subject _____

12. to worry about something all the time _____

13. compulsion by use of force or threats _____

14. rainy season accompanying seasonal wind _____

15. to break (a moral law) _____

22

16. a rich and powerful person _____

17. a generous giving, especially of money _____

18. a shallow lake or channel _____

19. a group of soldiers with a lieutenant in charge _____

20. to satirize or ridicule _____

WRITING SENTENCES

Use each new word in the box to write an original sentence.

lampoon	lagoon	monsoon	platoon	tycoon
largess	digress	duress	obsess	transgress

21. _____

22. _____

23. _____

24. _____

25. _____

26. _____

27. _____

28. _____

29. _____

30. _____

UNIT 4

MEMORY TIPS:

Word building with Roots, Prefixes, and Suffixes:

---

con	together; as *conductive*
di	apart, not; as *diminutive*
ion	act of; as *legion, fusion, precision, profusion, introversion*
ive	relating to; as *lucrative, abortive, conductive, cumulative, diminutive*

NEW WORDS

legion	fusion	precision	profusion	introversion
lucrative	abortive	conducive	cumulative	diminutive

1. LEGION ['lidʒən] *n.* a large group or number of people **rhyming sound –ion**

Each **legion** contained between 3000 to 6000 soldiers.

2. fusion ['fjuʒ(ə)n] *n.* melting; product of fusing; popular music blending styles

The **fusion** of copper and zinc makes the metal brass.

Word Families: **fusional** *adj.*

3. precision [prɪ'sɪʒ(ə)n] *n.* the quality of being accurate and exact; *adj.* accurate

Scientific instruments have to be made with great **precision**.

Word Families: **precisionism** *n.;* **precisionist** *n.*

4. profusion   [prə'fjuʒ(ə)n] *n.* a large quantity of something

Everything was there in such **profusion** that we did not know what to take.

5. introversion   [ˌɪntrə'vɚʒən] *n.* the condition of being folded inward; concern with one's

own thoughts and feelings

Of course, America went through a similar period of **introversion** after the Vietnam war.

6. LUCRATIVE ['lukrətɪv] *adj.* bringing a lot of money   **rhyming sound -ive**

Michael has found a **lucrative** job in a private equity firm in New York.

Word Families: **lucrativeness** *n.;* **lucratively** *adv.*

7. abortive   [ə'bɔrtɪv] *adj.* not finished therefore not successful

They had to abandon their **abortive** attempts to make airplanes.

Word Families: **abortively** *adv.*

8. conducive   [kən'dusɪv] *adj.* creating a situation that helps something to happen

Sometimes the home environment just isn't **conducive** to reading.

9. cumulative   ['kjumjələtɪv] *adj.* increasing steadily

The process of improvement is a **cumulative** one

Word Families: **cumulativeness** *n.;* **cumulatively** *adv.*

10. diminutive   [dɪ'mɪnjətɪv] *adj.* very short or small

The pretty woman was a **diminutive** figure beside her tall husband.

Word Families: **diminutiveness** *n.;* **diminutively** *adv.*

SENTENCE COMPLETION

Choose one of the new words to complete each sentence below. Make changes if necessary.

legion	fusion	precision	profusion	introversion
lucrative	abortive	conducive	cumulative	diminutive

1. In Spring, flowers are blooming in _____ in my front garden.

2. _____ instruments are used to help pilots in guiding their aircraft.

3. High energy environment are not _____ to the retention of organic matter in muds.

4. Her delightful sense of humor won her a _____ of friends on campus.

5. It would be an _____ effort to try to curb inflation this way.

6. His administration was plagued by one petty scandal after another, _____

   very damaging.

7. The contrast between extroversion and _____ is entirely superficial.

8. The actress has decided to turn her hobby into a _____ business.

9. His previous _____ of jazz, pop and African melodies have proved highly successful.

10. We noticed a _____ figure standing at the entrance.

DEFINITION MATCHING

Choose one of the new words to match each definition below.

legion	fusion	precision	profusion	introversion
lucrative	abortive	conducive	cumulative	diminutive

11. not finished therefore not successful _____

12. bringing a lot of money _____

13. melting; product of fusing _____

14. very short or small _____

15. very exact and accurate   _____

16. increasing steadily   _____

17. the condition of being folded inward   _____

18. a large group or number of people   _____

19. a situation that helps something to happen   _____

20. large quantity of something   _____

WRITING SENTENCES

Use each new word in the box to write an original sentence.

legion	fusion	precision	profusion	introversion
lucrative	abortive	conducive	cumulative	diminutive

21._____

22._____

23._____

24._____

25._____

26._____

27._____

28._____

29._____

30._____

UNIT 5

MEMORY TIPS:

Word building with Roots, Prefixes, and Suffixes:

---

ac	to; as *acrid*
for	before; as *forbid*
id	of, like; as *lurid, acrid, forbid, rigid*

NEW WORDS

lull	dull	gull	null	skull
lurid	rid	acrid	forbid	rigid

1. LULL   [lʌl] *n.* a quiet period during a very active or violent situation; *v.* to make someone relaxed enough to sleep   **rhyming sound –ull**

There was a **lull** in political violence after the election of the current president.

2. dull   [dʌl] *adj.* boring or not interesting; *v.* to make a feeling weaker

Life in a remote mountain village could be very **dull** sometimes.

Word Families: **dullness** *n;* **dullish** *adj.;* **dully** *adv.*

3. gull   [gʌl] *n..* a large black and white bird; someone who is easily tricked; *v.* to cheat or trick someone

The ivory **gull** often follows polar bears to feed on the remains of seal kills.

4. null   [nʌl] *adj.* with on value or effect; *n.* a zero; *v.* to cancel out or remove

A spokeswoman said the agreement had been declared **null** and void.

5. skull   [skʌl] *n.* the bones of the head; a person's head or his mind

The poor girl was rushed to the hospital and treated for a fractured **skull.**

6. LURID   ['lʊrɪd] *adj.* vivid in shocking detail, sensational; glaring in color   **rhyming sound -id**

The pretty girl always paints her toe nails a **lurid** red or orange.

Word Families: **luridness** *n.*; **luridly** *adv.*

7. rid   [rɪd] *v.* to clear or relieve (of)

It is not always easy to **rid** oneself of the bad habits.

8. acrid   ['ækrɪd] *adj.* pungent, bitter

There seems to be an **acrid** tone to your remarks.

Word Families: **acridity** *n.*; **acridly** *adv.*

9. forbid   [fə'bɪd] *v.* to tell somebody not to do or have something

Brazil's constitution **forbids** the military use of nuclear energy.

10. rigid   ['rɪdʒɪd] *adj.* not easily changed

Her **rigid** adherence to the rules made her very unpopular in the office.

Word Families: **rigidity** *n.*; **rigidness** *n.*; **rigidify** *v.*; **rigidly** *adv.*

SENTENCE COMPLETION

Choose one of the new words to complete each sentence below. Make changes if necessary.

lull	dull	gull	null	skull
lurid	rid	acrid	forbid	rigid

1. The actress will have to get _____ of the excess weight on her hips.

2. There was never a _____ moment when Jenny was with us.

3. The woman looked at the men in the bar with a smile both _____ and desolate.

4. The minister's revelations of financial corruption were _____ and highly exaggerated.

5. This is just the _____ before the storm.

6. It was useless to _____ children to play in the park.

7. You are not supposed to _____ your friends and relatives.

8. The old man fell out of his window and cracked his _____.

9. If no value can be read from the fact table for a member, the value for that member is set to _____.

10. The entrance examination was so _____ that half of the students were ruled out.

DEFINITION MATCHING

Choose one of the new words to match each definition below.

lull	dull	gull	null	skull
lurid	rid	acrid	forbid	rigid

11. vivid in shocking detail, sensational _____

12. to cancel out or remove (a force or effect) _____

13. pungent, bitter _____

14. to tell somebody not to do something _____

15. not easily changed _____

16. a quiet period during a violent situation _____

17. a person's head or his mind _____

18. to cheat or trick someone _____

19. to clear or relieve (of)   _____

20. boring or not interesting   _____

WRITING SENTENCES

Use each new word in the box to write an original sentence.

lull	dull	gull	null	skull
lurid	rid	acrid	forbid	rigid

21._____

22._____

23._____

24._____

25._____

26._____

27._____

28._____

29._____

30._____

UNIT 6

MEMORY TIPS:

Word building with Roots, Prefixes, and Suffixes:

---

con	together, fully; as *consign, conviction*
ion	condition or action; as *malediction, friction, addiction,*
	conviction, jurisdiction
mal	bad; as *malediction, malign*
re	back, again; as *resign*

NEW WORDS

malediction	friction	addiction	conviction	jurisdiction
malign	align	assign	consign	resign

1. MALEDICTION [ˌmælə'dɪkʃən] *n.* curse   **rhyming sound –iction**

It is said that Shakespeare's remains were guarded by a **malediction**.

Word Families: **maledictive** *adj.*; **maledictory** *adj.*

2. friction   ['frɪkʃ(ə)n] *n.* the fact that one thing rubs against another; disagreement

At any rate, **friction** always manifests itself as a force that opposes motion.

3. addiction   [ə'dɪkʃ(ə)n] *n.* a strong need to take illegal or harmful drugs; a strong desire to spend time doing something

The man's **addiction** to drugs propelled him towards a life of crime.

Word Families: **addict** *n.;* **addictive** *adj.;* **addicted** *adj.*

4. conviction   [kən'vɪkʃ(ə)n] *n.* firm belief; instance of being convicted

The woman appealed unsuccessfully against her **conviction** for murder.

Word Families: **convict** *n..;* **convict** *v.*

5. jurisdiction   [ˌdʒʊrɪs'dɪkʃ(ə)n] *n.* the right or power to make legal decisions; an area

where a legal system operates

The British police have no **jurisdiction** over foreign bank accounts.

6. MALIGN   [mə'laɪn] *adj.* causing harm; evil in influence or effect; *v.* slander or defame
rhyming sound -ign

In an institutional environment that demanded lying, more **malign** lies could flourish.

Word Families: **malignity** *n.;* **maligner** *n.;* **malignant** *adj.;* **malignly** *adv.*

7. align   [ə'laɪn] *v.* to bring (a person or group) into agreement with the policy of another; to play in a line

Conservatives, generally, were sure that Taft would **align** himself with the Old Guard in Congress.

8. assign   [ə'saɪn] *v.* to give someone a job to do; to put someone in a particular group

If you wish to **assign** students to the project, follow the instructions above.

Word Families: **assignment** *n.;* **assignor** *n.;* **assigner** *n.;* **assignable** *adj.*

9. consign   [kən'saɪn] *v.* to put somewhere; to send (goods)

For decades, many of Malevich's works were **consigned** to the basements of Soviet museums.

Word Families: **consignment** *n;* **consignee** *n.;* **consignor** *n..*

10. resign   [rɪ'zaɪn] *v.* to state formally that you are leaving a job permanently

The college president has **resigned** over claims he lied to get the job.

SENTENCE COMPLETION

Choose one of the new words to complete each sentence below. Make changes if necessary.

malediction	friction	addiction	conviction	jurisdiction
malign	align	assign	consign	resign

1. She underwent aversion therapy for her _____ to smoking.

2. He underscored the fact the ICC has no _____ over Sudan.

3. He was known to the police because of previous _____.

4. The politician was answered with a torrent of _____.

5. If she were to _____, who would take her position?

6. We will _____ the goods to him by express.

7. He likes to _____ innocent people.

8. Oil is put in machinery to reduce the _____.

9. When teachers _____ homework, students usually have an obligation to do it.

10. He has attempted to _____ the Socialists with the environmental movement.

DEFINITION MATCHING

Choose one of the new words to match each definition below.

malediction	friction	addiction	conviction	jurisdiction
malign	align	assign	consign	resign

11. to place in a line   _____

12. a strong need to take illegal or harmful drugs   _____

13. the power to make legal decisions   _____

14. to put somewhere, to send (goods)   _____

15. the fact that one thing rubs against another   _____

16. instance of being convicted   _____

17. to give up office, a job, etc.; to reconcile   _____

18. causing harm   _____

19. to give someone a job to do   _____

20. curse   _____

WRITING SENTENCES

Use each new word in the box to write an original sentence.

malediction	friction	addiction	conviction	jurisdiction
malign	align	assign	consign	resign

21._____

22._____

23._____

24._____

25._____

26._____

27._____

28._____

29._____

30._____

UNIT 7

MEMORY TIPS:

Word building with Roots, Prefixes, and Suffixes:

---

ary	one who, concerning; as *mercenary, adversary, centenary, mortuary, planetary*
cent	hundred; as *centenary*
ity	state or quality; as *materiality, brutality, fatality, formality, morality*

NEW WORDS

materiality	brutality	fatality	formality	morality
mercenary	adversary	centenary	mortuary	planetary

1. MATERIALITY [mə,tɪri'ælɪti] *n.* the quality of being physical; consisting of matter
rhyming sound –ality

In general, art expresses personal ideas while exploring **materiality** on a human scale.

2. brutality [bru'tæləti] *n.* extreme violence, especially when it is deliberately cruel

The woman accused the police of using unwarranted **brutality**.

Word Families: **brutal** *adj.;* **brutally** *adv.*

3. fatality [fə'tæləti] *n.* a death caused by an accident, war, violence, or disease

36

Drunk driving **fatalities** have declined dramatically over the past decade.

Word Families: **fatalities** *n. pl.;* **fatal** *adj.;* **fatally** *adv.*

4. formality   [fɔr'mæləti] *n.* requirement of custom or etiquette; necessary procedure without real importance

This is a **formality** we have to go through

Word Families: **formalities** *n.pl.;* **formal** *adj.;* **formally** *adv.*

5. morality   [mə'ræləti] *n.* principles of right or wrong behavior

They look like figures representing gluttony in a medieval **morality** play.

Word Families: **moralities** *n.pl..;* **moral** *adj.;* **morally** *adv.*

6. MERCENARY ['mɜrs(ə)n͵eri] *adj.* influenced by greed; *n.pl.* –aries hired soldiers
rhyming sound -icious

Mercenary men lust only for money and gains.

Word Families: **mercenaries** *n.pl.*

7. adversary   ['ædvər͵seri] *n.* an enemy or opponent

The mayor's political **adversaries** were creating a lot of trouble for him.

Word Families: **adversaries** *n.pl.*

8. centenary   ['sent(ə)n͵eri] *n.* a centennial

The university will celebrate its **centenary** next year!

Word Families: **centenaries** *n.pl.*

9. mortuary   ['mɔrtʃu͵eri] *n.* building where corpses are kept before burial or cremation

A medical institution shall place the corpse of a patient in the **mortuary** in time.

10. planetary   ['plænə͵teri] *adj.* relating to a planet or the planets

The sciences of **planetary** geology have benefited tremendously from these new finds.

SENTENCE COMPLETION

Choose one of the new words to complete each sentence below. Make changes if necessary.

materiality	brutality	fatality	formality	morality
mercenary	adversary	centenary	mortuary	planetary

1. Law and _____ are the bulwark of society.

2. This regiment was entirely composed of _____ troops

3. It is my conviction, or my delusion, that crime brings its own _____ with it.

4. You can rest assured that nothing has really happened in _____ here.

5. The poll was conducted as part of the Science Museum's events to mark

   its _____.

6. She didn't like the _____ of the party.

7. New discoveries about Uranus excited _____ astronomers in 1977.

8. The girl was not allowed to see her mother for the last time in the _____.

9. Her personal experience of men was of extreme violence and _____.

10. Both of the wrestlers tried to tumble the _____ with all their strength.

DEFINITION MATCHING

Choose one of the new words to match each definition below.

materiality	brutality	fatality	formality	morality
mercenary	adversary	centenary	mortuary	planetary

11. building where corpses are kept   _____

12. principles of right or wrong behavior   _____

13. relating to a planet or the planets   _____

14. death caused by an accident, war, or disease   _____

15. a centennial   _____

16. the quality of being physical   _____

17. hired soldiers   _____

18. an enemy or opponent   _____

19. extreme violence when it is deliberately cruel   _____

20. requirement of custom or etiquette   _____

WRITING SENTENCES

Use each new word in the box to write an original sentence.

materiality	brutality	fatality	formality	morality
mercenary	adversary	centenary	mortuary	planetary

21._____

22._____

23._____

24._____

25._____

26._____

27._____

28._____

29._____

30._____

UNIT 8

MEMORY TIPS:

Word building with Roots, Prefixes, and Suffixes:

---

ate	Verb: cause to be; as *mitigate, innate, emulate, oscillate, propagate*
ify	Verb: cause; as *mollify, edify, ossify, vilify, rectify*
in	into, in, on; as *innate*

NEW WORDS

mitigate	innate	emulate	oscillate	propagate
mollify	certify	ossify	vilify	rectify

1. MITIGATE   ['miti,geɪt] *v.* to reduce the harmful effects of something   **rhyming**

       sound –ate

       The doctor has found the ways to **mitigate** her pain.

       Word Families: **mitigator** *n.;* **mitigatory** *adj.;* **mitigatable** *adj.*

2. innate   ['ɪ,neɪt] *adj.* being part of someone's nature; inborn

       It seems to me that Americans have an **innate** sense of fairness.

       Word Families: **innateness** *n.;* **innately** *adv.*

3. emulate   ['emjə,leɪt] *v.* to attempt to equal by imitating

It was natural that he should **emulate** his brethren.

Word Families: **emulation** *n.;* **emulator** *n.;* **emulative** *adj.*

4. oscillate   ['ɑsɪˌleɪt] *v.* to swing back and forth

Oil markets **oscillated** on the day's reports from Geneva.

Word Families: **oscillation** *n. pl..;* **oscillatory** *adj.*

5. propagate   ['prɑpəˌgeɪt] *v.* to spread (information and ideas); to reproduce or breed

They **propagated** political doctrines which promised to drive economic growth.

Word Families: **propagation** *n.*; **propagative** *adj.*

6. MOLLIFY   ['mɑləˌfaɪ] *v.* to make someone less angry or upset   **rhyming sound -ify**

The investigation was undertaken primarily to **mollify** pressure groups.

Word Families: **mollification** *n.;* **mollifier** *n.*

7. certify   ['sɜrtɪˌfaɪ] *v.* to state officially that something is true or accurate

I **certify** this as a true copy of his letter.

8. ossify   ['ɑsɪˌfaɪ] *v.* to cause to become bone; to harden

British society tended to **ossify** and close ranks as the 1930s drew to their close.

Word Families: **ossification** *n.*

9. vilify   ['vɪləˌfaɪ] *v.* to attack the character of

He was **vilified**, hounded, and forced into exile by the FBI.

Word Families: **vilification** *n;* **vilifier** *n.*

10. rectify   ['rektəˌfaɪ] *v.* to correct a problem or mistake

Only an act of Congress could **rectify** the situation

Word Families: **rectification** *n.;* **rectifier** *n.*

SENTENCE COMPLETION

Choose one of the new words to complete each sentence below. Make changes if necessary.

mitigate	innate	emulate	oscillate	propagate
mollify	certify	ossify	vilify	rectify

1. On an oscilloscope, you can see an electrical current _____ up and down.

2. Governments should endeavor to _____ distress.

3. Jennifer tried every means to _____ her angry boss.

4. Missionaries went far afield to _____ their faith.

5. I _____ on my honor that she is innocent.

6. The girl obviously has an _____ talent for music.

7. Measures to increase ventilation will _____ the problem.

8. This disease will make her tendons _____ and her body paralyzed into a statue.

9. Mary did not deserve the _____ she had been subjected to.

10. It is customary for boys to _____ their fathers.

DEFINITION MATCHING

Choose one of the new words to match each definition below.

mitigate	innate	emulate	oscillate	propagate
mollify	certify	ossify	vilify	rectify

11. to attack the character of   _____

12. to correct a problem or mistake   _____

13. to harden   _____

14. being part of someone's nature; inborn   _____

15. to state officially that something is true   _____

16. to swing back and forth   _____

17. to attempt to equal by imitating   _____

18. to spread (information and ideas)   _____

19. to make someone less angry or upset   _____

20. to reduce the harmful effects of something   _____

WRITING SENTENCES

Use each new word in the box to write an original sentence.

mitigate	innate	emulate	oscillate	propagate
mollify	certify	ossify	vilify	rectify

21. _____

22. _____

23. _____

24. _____

25. _____

26. _____

27. _____

28. _____

29. _____

30. _____

UNIT 9

MEMORY TIPS:

Word building with Roots, Prefixes, and Suffixes:

---

ant	Adjective: a kind of agent, indication; as *mordant, penchant, petulant, rampant, recalcitrant*
dis	apart, not; as *dispose*
fore	before; as *foreclose*

NEW WORDS

mordant	penchant	petulant	rampant	recalcitrant
morose	compose	dispose	foreclose	verbose

1. MORDANT   ['mɔrd(ə)nt] *adj.* sarcastic or scathing; *n.* substance used to fix dyes
rhyming sound –ant

The senator's political opponents feared her **mordant** wit.

Word Families: **mordancy** *n.* ; **mordantly** *adv.*

2. penchant   ['penʃənt] *n.* a feeling of liking something very much

American pragmatism produces a **penchant** for examining issues separately.

3. petulant   ['petʃələnt] *n.* childishly irritable or peevish

44

The billionaire's daughter is sometimes wayward, **petulant**, and disagreeable.

Word Families: **petulance** *n.;* **petulantly** *adv.*

4. rampant ['ræmpənt] *adj.* existing, happening, or spreading in a uncontrolled way

Poverty and disease are **rampant** in rural areas of this country.

Word Families: **rampancy** *n.;* **rampantly** *adv.*

5. recalcitrant [rɪ'kælsɪtrənt] *adj.* refusing to obey orders

Besides, even for **recalcitrant** students, there are provisions under the current system to deal with them.

Word Families: **recalcitrance** *n.;* **recalcitrantly** *adv.*

6. MOROSE [mə'roʊs] *adj.* feeling unhappy; in a bad mood   **rhyming sound -ose**

The man became at times listless and **morose**.

7. compose [kəm'poʊz] *v.* to put together; to form something

The committee is **comprised** of representatives from both the public and private sectors.

8. dispose [dɪ'spoʊz] *v.* to place in a certain order; to make somebody willing or receptive to do something

The millionaire was forced to **dispose** of all his treasures.

Word Families: **disposal** *n.;* **disposed** *adj.;* **disposable** *adj.*

9. foreclose [fɔr'kloʊz] *v* to take possession of someone's property because he failed to pay back the money borrowed to buy it

The bank **foreclosed** on the mortgage for his previous home.

Word Families: **foreclosure** *n.*

10. verbose [vɜr'boʊs] *adj.* using more words than necessary, and therefore long

and boring

For the first time, her usually **verbose** husband was willing to listen.

SENTENCE COMPLETION

Choose one of the new words to complete each sentence below. Make changes if necessary.

mordant	penchant	petulant	rampant	recalcitrant
morose	compose	dispose	foreclose	verbose

1. They have an equal and opposite _____ for conspiracy theories.

2. Michael's speech carried a wicked and _____ sense of humor.

3. The girl had grown more than usually _____ and incalculable.

4. She greeted him now as though he were a _____ member of the family, rather

   than a menacing outsider.

5. His academic writings are usually difficult and _____.

6. Inevitably, many lenders will _____ on the homeowner.

7. These new internet billionaires look just like normal adults, but inside, they are
   _____, narcissistic children with oversized egos.

8. There was only a small part of his estate that Sir Walter could _____ of.

9. England, Scotland and Wales _____ the island of Great Britain.

10. Malaria is still _____ in some swampy regions.

DEFINITION MATCHING

Choose one of the new words to match each definition below.

mordant	penchant	petulant	rampant	recalcitrant
morose	compose	dispose	foreclose	verbose

11. childishly irritable or peevish   _____

12. using more words than necessary   _____

13. to take possession of someone's property   _____

14. refusing to obey orders   _____

15. to make somebody willing to do something   _____

16. sarcastic or scathing   _____

17. feeling unhappy, in a bad mood   _____

18. to form something   _____

19. a feeling of liking something very much   _____

20. existing or happening in a uncontrolled way   _____

WRITING SENTENCES

Use each new word in the box to write an original sentence.

mordant	penchant	petulant	rampant	recalcitrant
morose	compose	dispose	foreclose	verbose

21. _____

22. _____

23. _____

24. _____

25. _____

26. _____

27. _____

28. _____

29. _____

30. _____

UNIT 10

MEMORY TIPS:

Word building with Roots, Prefixes, and Suffixes:

---

con	together; as *consent*
in	not; as *insane*
pro	forward, before; as *profane*

NEW WORDS

mundane	**humane**	**insane**	**profane**	**hurricane**
munificent	**consent**	**extent**	**aliment**	**regiment**

1. MUNDANE [mʌn'deɪn] *adj.* ordinary and not interesting; relating to the world and

practical matters   **rhyming sound –ane**

It was hard to return to **mundane** matters after such a wonderful trip.

Word Families: **mundanity** *n.;* **mundaneness** *n.;* **mundanely** *adv.*

2. humane   [hju'meɪn] *adj.* kind or merciful

Our aim is for a more just and **humane** society.

Word Families: **humaneness** n.; **humanely** *adv.*

3. insane   [ɪn'seɪn] *adj.* very stupid or crazy; suffering from severe mental illness

Joanne would be **insanely** jealous if Bill left her for another woman.

Word Families: **insanely** *adj.*

4. profane [prəˈfeɪn] *adj.* showing a lack of respect for God or religion; *v.* to show a lack of respect for God or religion

To smoke in a church or mosque would be a **profane** act.

Word Families: **profanation** *n.;* **profanity** *n.;.***profanely** *adv.*

5. hurricane [ˈhʌrɪˌkeɪn] *n.* a violent storm with strong wind and heavy rain

During the **hurricane**, many people's homes were destroyed.

Word Families: **hurricanes** *n.pl.*

6. MUNIFICENT [mjuˈnɪfɪsənt] *adj.* extremely generous　　**rhyming sound -ent**

Dunn is one of the country's most **munificent** artistic benefactors.

Word Families: **munificence** *n.;* **munificently** *adv.*

7. consent [kənˈsent] *v.* to give approval for something; *n.* permission to do something

To be able to go on a field trip, a written **consent** of the parent is required.

8. extent [ɪkˈstent] *n.* range over which something extends, the size or area

The city government itself has little information on the **extent** of industrial pollution in the region.

Word Families: **extents** *n.pl.*

9. aliment [ˈæləmənt] *n.* something that feeds or sustains something else

Can we find the mystic **aliment** that would give them vigor?

Word Families: **aliments** *n.pl.*

10. regiment [ˈredʒɪmənt] *n.* organized body of troops as a unit of the army

The **regiment** secured its position to attack the enemy.

Word Families: **regimentation** *n.;* **regimental** *adj.*

SENTENCE COMPLETION

Choose one of the new words to complete each sentence below. Make changes if necessary.

mundane	humane	insane	profane	hurricane
munificent	consent	extent	aliment	regiment

1. For an instant, the man became _____, a screaming animal.

2. Nancy is one of the most _____ girls I have ever known.

3. The full _____ of the losses was disclosed yesterday.

4. Everyone has to learn how to do _____ tasks well.

5. The advancement of science and technology is the best _____ to a better society.

6. The _____ blew with such force that trees were uprooted.

7. Mary finally _____ to donate five thousand dollars to the United Way.

8. As he hated the war in Vietnam, Michael decided to desert his _____.

9. These people have _____ the long upheld traditions of the Church.

10. Certainly those who spread the message of God are the most _____.

DEFINITION MATCHING

Choose one of the new words to match each definition below.

mundane	humane	insane	profane	hurricane
munificent	consent	extent	aliment	regiment

11. organized body of troops as a unit of the army   _____

12. permission to do something   _____

13. something that feeds or sustains something else   _____

14. to show a lack of respect for God or religion   _____

15. the size or area of something   _____

16. ordinary and not interesting   _____

17. a violent storm with strong wind and heavy rain _____

18. kind and merciful   _____

19. extremely generous   _____

20. very stupid or crazy   _____

WRITING SENTENCES

Use each new word in the box to write an original sentence.

mundane	humane	insane	profane	hurricane
munificent	consent	extent	aliment	regiment

21._____

22._____

23._____

24._____

25._____

26._____

27._____

28._____

29._____

30._____

UNIT 11

MEMORY TIPS:

Word building with Roots, Prefixes, and Suffixes:

---

ious	characterized by; as *nefarious, vicarious, precarious,* *multifarious, temerarious*
mult	many; as *multifarious*
pre	before; as *precarious*
tele	distance; as *telekinesis*

NEW WORDS

nefarious	precarious	vicarious	multifarious	temerarious
nemesis	thesis	mimesis	exegesis	telekinesis

1. NEFARIOUS [nɪˈferiəs] *adj.* evil or dishonest   **rhyming sound –arious**

The man was universally feared because of his many **nefarious** deeds.

Word Families: **nefariousness** *n.;* **nefariously** *adj.*

2. precarious [prɪˈkeriəs] *adj.* likely to change or become dangerous without warning

The company's financial situation has become **precarious**.

Word Families: **precariousness** *n.;* **precariously** *adv.*

3. vicarious [vɪˈkeriəs] *adj.* experienced through the actions of other people

Many young people use television as their **vicarious** form of social life.

Word Families: **vicariousness** *n.;* **vicariously** *adv.*

4. multifarious   [ˌmʌltɪ'feriəs] *adj.* consisting of many different types

Chapter five elaborates territorial states and the **multifarious** cultures.
Word Families: **multifariousness** *n.;* **multifariously** *adv.*

5. temerarious   [ˌtɛmə'rɛriəs] *adj.* showing a reckless confidence that may be offensive

Some people are just **temerarious** enough to break the rules for their own sake.

Word Families: **temerariously** *adj.*

6. NEMESIS   ['neməsɪs] *n.*retribution or vengeance   **rhyming sound -esis**

Some people believe that AIDS is our collective **nemesis**.

Word Families: **nemeses** *n.pl.*

7. thesis   ['θiːsis] *n.* written work submitted for a degree

The fundamental **thesis** of this book goes back to the winter of 1969.

Word Families: **theses** *n.pl.*

8. mimesis   [mɪ'misɪs] *n.* acting without the use of words; a rhetorical use of what somebody else might have said

Fictionality and **mimesis** are common in novels.

9. exegesis   [ˌeksə'dʒisɪs] *n.* explanation of a text, especially. the Bible

Within this context, Fraser is capable of **exegesis** that goes beyond

the obvious.

Word Families: **exegetic** *adj.;* **exegetical** *adj.*

10. telekinesis   [ˌtelɪkɪ'nisɪs] *n.* the power to move or change objects using your mind

Telekinesis is another ability for which there is little hard evidence.

Word Families: **telekinetic** *adj.*

SENTENCE COMPLETION

Choose one of the new words to complete each sentence below. Make changes if necessary.

nefarious	precarious	vicarious	multifarious	temerarious
nemesis	thesis	mimesis	exegesis	telekinesis

1. A soldier leads a very _____ life.

2. How often we have been _____ and rushed unwisely in.

3. The reasons for closure are _____.

4. The uncanny girl invented fantasy lives for her own _____ pleasure.

5. The playwright uses _____ in his plays.

6. In 1946, General Electric was fined by the American government owing to its _____ wartime activities.

7. Yet the imminent crisis in its balance of payments may be the President's _____.

8. Johnson was awarded his Master of Arts degree for his _____ on Keats.

9. The old man has the ability to manipulate and use magic items via _____.

10. Biblical _____ was a phase of the rational approach to religion that was popular in the Age of Reason.

DEFINITION MATCHING

Choose one of the new words to match each definition below.

nefarious	precarious	vicarious	multifarious	temerarious
nemesis	thesis	mimesis	exegesis	telekinesis

11. the power to move objects using your mind   _____

12. consisting of many different types   _____

13. to become dangerous without warning   _____

14. explanation of a text, especially. the Bible   _____

15. acting without the use of words   _____

16. evil or dishonest   _____

17. written work submitted for a degree   _____

18. showing a confidence that may be offensive   _____

19. retribution or vengeance   _____

20. experienced through the actions of other people   _____

WRITING SENTENCES

Use each new word in the box to write an original sentence.

nefarious	precarious	vicarious	multifarious	temerarious
nemesis	thesis	mimesis	exegesis	telekinesis

21._____

22._____

23._____

24._____

25._____

26._____

27._____

28._____

29._____

30._____

UNIT 12

MEMORY TIPS:

Word building with Roots, Prefixes, and Suffixes:

ic	of, like; as *neoteric, generic, numeric, atmospheric, esoteric*
neo	new; as *neophyte, neoteric*
pro	forward, before; as *proselyte*

NEW WORDS

neophyte	byte	acolyte	proselyte	troglodyte
neoteric	generic	numeric	atmospheric	esoteric

1. NEOPHYTE ['niə‚faɪt] *n.* someone who is just learning to do something and doesn't have much experience   **rhyming sound –yte**

She is just a **neophyte** in politics.

Word Families: **neophytes** *n.pl.*

2. byte [baɪt] *n.* a basic unit for storing computer information, a byte is approximately equivalent to one printed character

They are intended for character sets where a character does not fit into a single **byte**.

Word Families: **bytes** *n.pl.*

3. acolyte ['ækə‚laɪt] *n.* someone who helps an important person

To her **acolytes**, Helen Johnson is just known as "Dragon Lady.".

Word Families: **acolytes** *n. pl.*

4. proselyte   ['prɑsə,laɪt] *n..* a new convert to a religious faith or political doctrine

We should allow **proselytes** to enter no matter where they are from.

Word Families: **proselytism** *n.*

5. troglodyte   ['trɑglə,daɪt] *n.* cave dweller

He dismissed advocates of a completely free market as economic **troglodytes** with no concern for the social consequences.

Word Families: **troglodytes** *n.pl.*

6. NEOTERIC   [,niə'tɛrɪk] *adj.* having a contemporary origin   **rhyming sound -eric**

Our products are famous for **neoteric** design and fine craftsmanship.

7. generic   [dʒə'nerɪk] *adj.* of a class, group, or genus

The doctor offered me a choice of a branded or a generic drug.

Word Families: **generics** *n.pl.;* **genrically** *adv.*

8. numeric   [nu'mɛrɪk] *adj.* numerical

The instructions of the program have to be written in a **numeric** form

Word Families: **numerically** *adv.*

9. atmospheric   [,ætmə'sferɪk] *adj.* relating to or existing in the atmosphere around the earth or another planet

The barometer marked a continuing fall in **atmospheric** pressure.

Word Families: **atmospherical** *adj.;* **atmospherically** *adv..*

10. esoteric   [,esə'terɪk] *adj.* known about or understood by very few people

The quantum theory is not just an **esoteric** addendum.

Word Families: **esotericism** *n.;* **esotericist** *n.;* **esoterically** *adv.*

SENTENCE COMPLETION

Choose one of the new words to complete each sentence below. Make changes if necessary.

neophyte	byte	acolyte	proselyte	troglodyte
neoteric	generic	numeric	atmospheric	esoteric

1. _____ nuclear tests are now banned by an international treaty.

2. The old man is a _____ who doesn't know anything about city life.

3. There are indications that his _____ popularity may be ebbing.

4. They discussed about the possibility of establishing _____ Christian schools in Japan.

5. David was no _____ and had no fancies about the business.

6. A _____ is the smallest unit of processing in any computer architecture.

7. Jenny Houston, an _____ of the U.S. senator, wrote the famous speech on women's rights.

8. The woman is a _____ of the new political party.

9. They encourage doctors to prescribe cheaper _____ drugs instead of more expensive brand names.

10. Do you want to use your _____ keypad instead of the mouse?

DEFINITION MATCHING

Choose one of the new words to match each definition below.

neophyte	byte	acolyte	proselyte	troglodyte
neoteric	generic	numeric	atmospheric	esoteric

11. the cave dweller   _____

12. known about or understood by very few people _____

13. someone who helps an important person _____

14. having a contemporary origin _____

15. someone who is just learning to do something _____

16. relating to atmosphere around the earth _____

17. numerical _____

18. a basic unit for storing computer information _____

19. of a class, group, or genus _____

20. a new convert to a religion or political doctrine _____

WRITING SENTENCES

Use each new word in the box to write an original sentence.

neophyte	byte	acolyte	proselyte	troglodyte
neoteric	generic	numeric	atmospheric	esoteric

21. _____

22. _____

23. _____

24. _____

25. _____

26. _____

27. _____

28. _____

29. _____

30. _____

UNIT 13

MEMORY TIPS:

Word building with Roots, Prefixes, and Suffixes:

---

ard	characterized by; as *niggard, bard, discard, retard, safeguard*
dis	apart, not; as *discard*
re	back, again; as *retard*
un	not; as *unsettle*

NEW WORDS

nettle	fettle	mettle	settle	unsettle
niggard	bard	discard	retard	safeguard

1. NETTLE   ['net(ə)l] *n.* plant with stinging hairs on the leaves; *v.* to annoy someone
rhyming sound –ettle

Michael was **nettled** by her rude manners.

Word Families: **nettled** *adj.*

2. fettle   ['fet(ə)l] *n.* state of health or spirits

She was in fine **fettle** when she returned from her trip to Paris.

3. mettle   ['met(ə)l] *n.* the determination and ability to deal with problems

For both sides, it's the first real test of their **mettle** this season.

Word Families: **mettlesome** *adj.*

4. settle   ['set(ə)l] *n.* a long wooden bench with high back and arms; *v.* to arrange or put in order; to become established as a resident

In an attempt to **settle** the case, Mike has agreed to make full resitution.

Word Families: **settleable** *adj.*

5. unsettle   [ʌn'set(ə)l] *v.* to make someone feel nervous, confused, or upset

The uncertainty is likely to **unsettle** the capital market.

Word Families: **unsettlement n.; unsettlingly** *adv.*

6. NIGGARD   ['nɪgəd] *n.* somebody regarded as stingy or miserly   **rhyming**

sound -ard

Never have we seen such a **niggard** like him!

Word Families: **niggardly** *adj.*

7. bard   [bɑrd] *n.* a poet

Byron was her favourite **bard** from the period when she first could feel.
Word Families: **bards** *n.pl.* **bardic** *adj.*

8. discard   [dɪs'kɑrd] *v.* to get rid of something you no longer want

He **discards** his winter underclothing when the weather gets warm.

Word Families: **discardable** *adj.*

9. retard   ['ri,tɑrd] *v.* to delay or slow (process or development)

That unpleasant news might **retard** her recovery

Word Families: retardation n.; **retarded** *adj.*

10. safeguard   ['seɪf,gɑrd] *v.* to protect; *n.* protection

The first duty of a government is to **safeguard** its people against external aggression.

Word Families: **safeguards** *n.pl.*

SENTENCE COMPLETION

Choose one of the new words to complete each sentence below. Make changes if necessary.

nettle	fettle	mettle	settle	unsettle
niggard	bard	discard	retard	safeguard

1. At first sight, the economy hit the August turmoil in fine _____.

2. Sooner or later, they will have to grasp the _____.

3. We may _____ all apprehensions for the safety of the Union.

4. Nature is prodigal in variety, but _____ in innovation.

5. Continuing violence will _____ negotiations over the country's future.

6. This was one of the first areas to be _____ by Europeans.

7. A system like ours lacks adequate _____ for civil liberties.

8. The girl showed her _____ by winning the contest in spite of her being handicapped.

9. The young _____ wandered all over the country in search of his love.

10. Nothing can _____ his resolution.

DEFINITION MATCHING

Choose one of the new words to match each definition below.

nettle	fettle	mettle	settle	unsettle
niggard	bard	discard	retard	safeguard

11. to delay or slow   _____

12. to become established as a resident   _____

13. to protect _____

14. to make someone feel nervous or upset _____

15. to get rid of something you no longer want _____

16. to annoy someone _____

17. a poet _____

18. a stingy person _____

19. determination and ability to deal with problems _____

20. state of health or spirits _____

WRITING SENTENCES

Use each new word in the box to write an original sentence.

nettle	fettle	mettle	settle	unsettle
niggard	bard	discard	retard	safeguard

21. _____

22. _____

23. _____

24. _____

25. _____

26. _____

27. _____

28. _____

29. _____

30. _____

UNIT 14

MEMORY TIPS:

Word building with Roots, Prefixes, and Suffixes:

---

de	down, away, from, about; as *defamatory*
ious	characterized by; as *noxious, precious, licentious, obnoxious, ostentatious*
ob	against; as *obnoxious*
ory	a place for; as *purgatory*

NEW WORDS

noxious	precious	nutritious	obnoxious	ostentatious
nugatory	mandatory	purgatory	signatory	defamatory

1. NOXIOUS   ['nɑkʃəs] *adj.* harmful or poisonous   **rhyming sound –ious**

Heavy industry pollutes our rivers with **noxious** chemicals.

Word Families: **noxiousness** *n.*; **noxiously** *adv.*

2. precious   ['preʃəs] *adj.* worth of great value and importance; loved and treasured

Water is becoming an increasingly precious resource.

Word Families: **preciously** *adj.*

3. nutritious   [nu'trɪʃəs] *adj.* nourishing

It is always important to choose enjoyable and **nutritious** foods.

Word Families: **nutrition** *n.;* **nutritiously** *adv.*

4. obnoxious   [ab'nakʃəs] *adj.* very rude. offensive, or unpleasant

It seemed as if the lawyer was deliberately being as **obnoxious** as possible.

Word Families: **obnoxiously** *adv.*

5. ostentatious   [ˌastɛn'teʃəs] *adj.* showy; pretentiously displaying

Obviously he had plenty of money and was generous in its use without being **ostentatious**.

Word Families: **ostentation** *n.;* **ostentatiously** *adv.*

6. NUGATORY   ['nugə,tɔri] *adj.* not important or effective   **rhyming sound -atory**

Her efforts have been totally **nugatory**.

Word Families: **nugatorily** *adv.*

7. mandatory   ['mændə,tɔri] *adj.* ordered by a law or rule; *n.* mandatary

The **mandatory** retirement age is 65 in most countries.

Word Families: **mandatories** *n.pl.*; **mandatorily** *adv.*

8. purgatory   ['pɜrgə,tɔri] *n.* a place where a penitent souls are purified; an unpleasant place or experience

It is like living in a **purgatory** over here in the big city.

Word Families: **purgatories** *n.pl.;* **purgatorial** *adj.*

9. signatory   ['sɪgnə,tɔri] *n.* one of the parties who signs a document

Both parties are **signatories** to the Joint Venture Agreement..

Word Families: **signatories** *n.pl.*

10. defamatory   [dɪ'fæmə,tɔri] *adj* .attacking the good reputation of

The company claimed that Google was liable as a publisher of **defamatory** comments.

Word Families: **defamation** *n.*

SENTENCE COMPLETION

Choose one of the new words to complete each sentence below. Make changes if necessary.

noxious	precious	nutritious	obnoxious	ostentatious
nugatory	mandatory	purgatory	signatory	defamatory

1. Kiwifruit is delicious and _____.

2. Actors, he decided, were too _____ and neurotic.

3. The people at my table were so _____ I simply had to change my seat.

4. _____ gases had built up in the sewer.

5. Any concession made to one _____ country has to be extended to all.

6. For me it was just a transfer from one _____ to another.

7. This is absolutely _____ to worry about the future.

8. That article about the mayor was completely _____.

9. The millionaire's daughter is absolutely not an _____ person anyway.

10. It is _____ for blood banks to test all donated blood for the virus.

DEFINITION MATCHING

Choose one of the new words to match each definition below.

noxious	precious	nutritious	obnoxious	ostentatious
nugatory	mandatory	purgatory	signatory	defamatory

11. very rude, offensive, or unpleasant   _____

12. an unpleasant place or experience   _____

13. nourishing   _____

14. one of the parties who signs a document   _____

15. ordered by a law or rule   _____

16. harmful or poisonous   _____

17. attacking the good reputation of   _____

18. showy   _____

19. not important or effective   _____

20. worth of great value and importance   _____

WRITING SENTENCES

Use each new word in the box to write an original sentence.

noxious	precious	nutritious	obnoxious	ostentatious
nugatory	mandatory	purgatory	signatory	defamatory

21. _____

22. _____

23. _____

24. _____

25. _____

26. _____

27. _____

28. _____

29. _____

30. _____

UNIT 15

MEMORY TIPS:

Word building with Roots, Prefixes, and Suffixes:

---

ance	state of; as *obeisance, askance, enhance, nuance, renaissance*
ate	cause to be; as *obfuscate, castigate, articulate, articulate, inveterate*
in	in, into, on; as *inveterate*
re	back, again; as *renaissance*

NEW WORDS

obeisance	askance	enhance	nuance	renaissance
obfuscate	castigate	deprecate	articulate	inveterate

1. OBEISANCE [oʊˈbeɪsəns] *n.* attitude of respect; bow or curtsy   **rhyming sound –ance**

She made a deep **obeisance** to the Queen.

Word Families: **obeisances** *n. pl.;* **obeisant** *adj.*

2. askance   [əˈskæns] *adv.* with doubt or suspicion

Asian policymakers are entitled to look **askance** at foreign bondholders.

3. enhance   [ɪnˈhæns] *v..* to improve something or make it more attractive

Good language skills should **enhance** your chances of getting a job.

Word Families: **enhancement** *n.;* **enhancer** *n.*

4. nuance   ['nu͵ɑns] *n.* subtle difference in color, meaning, or tone

With the slightest perceptible **nuance** he opened the way for bribery.

Word Families: **nuances** *n. pl.*

5. renaissance   [rɪ'neɪsəns] *n.* revival or rebirth; revival of learning in the 14-16 centuries

Humanism is definitely the essence of **renaissance**.

6. OBFUSCATE   ['ɑbfə͵skeɪt] *v.* to deliberately make something confusing or difficult to understand   **rhyming sound -ate**

They are **obfuscating** the issue, as only insurance companies can.

Word Families: **obfuscation** *n.;* **obfuscatory** *adj.*

7. castigate   ['kæstɪ͵geɪt] *v.* to criticize someone or something severely

The woman **castigated** her husband for being stupid and lazy.

Word Families: **castigation** *n.;* **castigator** *n.;* **castigatory** *adj.*

8. deprecate   ['deprə͵keɪt] *v.* to criticize something strongly

I strongly **deprecate** the use of violence by the students.

Word Families: **deprecation** *n.;* **deprecatory** *adj.;* **deprecatingly** *adv.*

9. articulate   [ɑr'tɪkjuleɪt] *adj.* able to express oneself clearly and coherently; *v.* to speak or say clearly and coherently

She was unable to offer an **articulate** description of what had happened.

Word Families: **articulation** *n;* **articulately** *adv.*

10. inveterate   [ɪn'vetərət] *adj.* firmly established in a habit or condition

Besides that, not all Americans are **inveterate** huggers anyway.

Word Families: **inveteracy** *n.;* **inveterately** *adv.*

SENTENCE COMPLETION

Choose one of the new words to complete each sentence below. Make changes if necessary.

obeisance	askance	enhance	nuance	renaissance
obfuscate	castigate	deprecate	articulate	inveterate

1. Florence is known as the shrine of _____.

2. He loved the _____ of joy that crossed her face when he touched her.

3. Marx never lost an opportunity to _____ colonialism.

4. When he was rich and powerful, all paid _____ to him.

5. The man failed to _____ what he really wanted to achieve in his startup.

6. Food is there to keep you healthy and _____ your enjoyment of life.

7. Michael was not only an avid reader but also an _____ note-taker.

8. They looked _____ at her and didn't know what to do.

9. Ethiopia rejected the verdict, and has since used diplomatic verbiage to _____ and stall.

10. The fashion now is to _____ the positive contributions of Keynesian economics.

DEFINITION MATCHING

Choose one of the new words to match each definition below.

obeisance	askance	enhance	nuance	renaissance
obfuscate	castigate	deprecate	articulate	inveterate

11. to criticize someone or something severely _____

12. to criticize something strongly _____

13. to improve something _____

14. to speak clearly and coherently _____

15. firmly established in a habit or condition   _____

16. attitude of respect   _____

17. to deliberately make something confusing   _____

18. subtle difference in color, meaning, or tone   _____

19. revival or rebirth   _____

20. with doubt or suspicion   _____

WRITING SENTENCES

Use each new word in the box to write an original sentence.

obeisance	askance	enhance	nuance	renaissance
obfuscate	castigate	deprecate	articulate	inveterate

21._____

22._____

23._____

24._____

25._____

26._____

27._____

28._____

29._____

30._____

UNIT 16

MEMORY TIPS:

Word building with Roots, Prefixes, and Suffixes:

---

apt	fit; as *aptitude*
ate	cause to be; as *objurgate, enunciate, exculpate, extrapolate, facilitate*
ob	against; as *objurgate, obtrude*
tude	state of; as *obtrude, delude, aptitude, lassitude, rectitude*

NEW WORDS

objurgate	enunciate	exculpate	extrapolate	facilitate
obtrude	delude	aptitude	lassitude	rectitude

1. OBJURGATE ['ɑbdʒɚ,get] *v.* to scold somebody angrily   **rhyming sound –ate**

She **objurgated** him for his insensitive remarks about the homeless people.

Word Families: **objurgation** *n.;* **objurgatory** *adj.*

2. enunciate   [ɪ'nʌnsi,et] *v.* to pronounce clearly; to utter; to claim

He is always willing to **enunciate** his opinions about politics clearly.

Word Families: **enunciation** *n;* **enunciator** *n.;* **enunciative** *adj.*

3. exculpate   ['ekskʌl,peɪt] *v.* to prove that someone is not guilty of a crime or bad action

Jack finally **exculpated** himself from a charge of theft in the bookstore.

Word Families: **exculpation** *n.;* **exculpatory** *n.;* **exculpatory** *adj.*

4. extrapolate [ɪk'stræpə,leɪt] *v.* to infer (something not known) from the know facts

Extrapolating from his findings, he reckons about 80% of these deaths might be attributed to smoking.

Word Families: **extrapolation** *n.;* **extrapolator** *n.;* **extrapolative** *adj.*

5. facilitate [fə'sɪlə,teɪt] *v.* to make it possible or easier for something to happen

I believe that this will **facilitate** our settlement of the matter.

Word Families: **facilitation** *n.;* **facilitator** *n.;* **facilitative** *adj.*

6. OBTRUDE [ɑb'trud] *v.* to push oneself or one's ideas on others **rhyming**

sound -ude

He didn't want to **obtrude** on her privacy.

Word Families: **obtrusion** *n.;* **obtruder** *n.;* **obtrusive** *adj.*

7. delude [dɪ'lud] *v.* to make someone think something is not true

Don't be deluded into thinking that we are out of danger yet.

Word Families: **delusion** *n.;* **deluder** *n.;* **deludedly** *adv.*

8. aptitude ['æptɪ,tud] *n.* natural ability that makes it easy for you to do something well

The girl showed a natural **aptitude** for painting.

Word Families: **aptitudes** *n.pl.*

9. lassitude ['læsɪ,tud] *n.* tiredness and lack of energy

In general, symptoms of anemia include general fatigue and **lassitude**.

10. rectitude ['rektɪ,tud] *n.* a very moral and correct way of behaving

The President is normally considered to be a man of the utmost moral **rectitude**.

SENTENCE COMPLETION

Choose one of the new words to complete each sentence below. Make changes if necessary.

objurgate	enunciate	exculpate	extrapolate	facilitate
obtrude	delude	aptitude	lassitude	rectitude

1. Forecasters can _____ the graph's future and then bet on the prediction.

2. Television _____ you into thinking you have experienced reality, when you haven't.

3. You should never _____ your opinions on others.

4. She is always willing to _____ her views to anyone who would listen.

5. It appears to me that some students have natural _____ for mathematics.

6. She was indignant with his presumption, self-satisfaction, and conscious _____.

7. The woman was _____ from the charge of murder.

8. A deadly _____ had taken hold of him.

9. Tom _____ her girl friend for being cruel to animals.

10. Thus, we shall obtain some illustrative materials which will _____ the understanding of the definition.

DEFINITION MATCHING

Choose one of the new words to match each definition below.

objurgate	enunciate	exculpate	extrapolate	facilitate
obtrude	delude	aptitude	lassitude	rectitude

11. natural ability to do something well   _____

12. a very moral and correct way of behaving   _____

13. tiredness and lack of energy   _____

14. infer something unknown from the known fact   _____

15. to make someone think that something is true   _____

16. to scold somebody angrily   _____

17. to make it possible for something to happen   _____

18. to prove that someone is not guilty of a crime   _____

19. to push oneself or one's ideas on others   _____

20. to pronounce clearly; to utter; to claim   _____

WRITING SENTENCES

Use each new word in the box to write an original sentence.

objurgate	enunciate	exculpate	extrapolate	facilitate
obtrude	delude	aptitude	lassitude	rectitude

21. _____

22. _____

23. _____

24. _____

25. _____

26. _____

27. _____

28. _____

29. _____

30. _____

UNIT 17

MEMORY TIPS:

Word building with Roots, Prefixes, and Suffixes:

arch	first, chief; as *oligarchy, anarchy, monarchy, hierarchy, patriarchy*
dis	apart, not; as *disputatious*
fort	strong; as *fortuitous*
ous, ious	characterized by; as *odious, fractious, facetious, fortuitous, disputatious*

NEW WORDS

odious	fractious	facetious	fortuitous	disputatious
oligarchy	anarchy	monarchy	hierarchy	patriarchy

1. ODIOUS   ['oʊdiəs] *adj.* very unpleasant   **rhyming sound –ous**

Brad is certainly the most **odious** man I have ever seen.

Word Families: **odiousness** *n.*; **odiously** *adv.*

2. fractious   ['frækʃəs] *adj.* easily upset or annoyed

That may make the world a little less **fractious**.

Word Families: **fractiousness** *n.;* **fractiously** *adv.*

3. facetious   [fə'siʃəs] *adj.* trying to be funny in a way that is not appropriate

Does George Bush possess a disarming grin, or a **facetious** smirk?

Word Families: **facetiousness** *n.;* **facetiously** *adv.*

4. fortuitous [fɔr'tuɪtəs] *adj.* happening by chance

His success is the result of a **fortuitous** combination of circumstances.

Word Families: **fortuitousness** *n.;* **fortuitously** *adv.*

5. disputatious [ˌdɪspjə'teʃəs] *adj.* tending to dispute or argue without adequate cause

She is the most **disputatious** girl in our class.

Word Families: **disputatiousness** *n.;* **disputatiously** *adv.*

6. OLIGARCHY ['alɪˌgɑrki] *n.* government by a small group of people; state governed this way **rhyming sound -archy**

The small county was ruled by an **oligarchy** that had no concern for the welfare of the people.

Word Families: **oligarchic** *adj.;* **oligarchical** *adj.;* **oligarchically** *adv.*

7. anarchy ['ænərki] *n.* lawlessness and disorder

Civil war and famine sent the nation plunging into **anarchy**.

8. monarchy ['mɑnərki] *n.* government by or a state ruled by a sovereign

By 1180 the native **Monarchy** of Ireland had gone to pieces.

Word Families: **monarchies** *n.pl.*

9. hierarchy ['haɪəˌrɑrki] *n.* people or things arranged in a graded order

There is a kind of social **hierarchy** even in this remote mountain village.

Word Families: **hierarchization** *n;* **hierarchic** *adj.*

10. patriarchy ['peɪtriˌɑrki] *n.* a society in which men have most of the power

That's not very different from what **patriarchy** always says about women.

Word Families: **patriarchies** *n.pl.*

SENTENCE COMPLETION

Choose one of the new words to complete each sentence below. Make changes if necessary.

odious	fractious	facetious	fortuitous	disputatious
oligarchy	anarchy	monarchy	hierarchy	patriarchy

1. He had worked with the diverse, _____ Iraqi opposition.

2. There is a rigid _____ of power in that country.

3. There was a protest against imperialism and _____ in the region

4. This place has an _____ smell; something must be rotten.

5. The main cause of women's and children's oppression is _____.

6. There would be _____ if we had no police.

7. She kept interrupting our discussion with _____ remarks.

8. Thomas is a strong supporter of the _____.

9. No one likes to be associated with a _____ and arrogant person.

10. A series of _____ circumstances advanced her career.

DEFINITION MATCHING

Choose one of the new words to match each definition below.

odious	fractious	facetious	fortuitous	disputatious
oligarchy	anarchy	monarchy	hierarchy	patriarchy

11. lawlessness and disorder   _____

12. people or things arranged in a graded order   _____

13. trying to be funny in a way that is not appropriate   _____

14. happening by chance   _____

15. a society in which men have most of the power   _____

16. very unpleasant   _____

17. government by a small group of people   _____

18. government by or a state ruled by a sovereign   _____

19. easily upset or annoyed   _____

20. tending to argue without adequate cause   _____

WRITING SENTENCES

Use each new word in the box to write an original sentence.

odious	fractious	facetious	fortuitous	disputatious
oligarchy	anarchy	monarchy	hierarchy	patriarchy

21. _____

22. _____

23. _____

24. _____

25. _____

26. _____

27. _____

28. _____

29. _____

30. _____

UNIT 18

MEMORY TIPS:

Word building with Roots, Prefixes, and Suffixes:

---

escent   becoming; as *putrescent, adolescent, opalescent*

ous, ious   characterized by; as *opprobrious, captious, horrendous,*

                     lecherous, mellifluous

NEW WORDS

opalescent	ferment	fervent	putrescent	adolescent
opprobrious	captious	horrendous	lecherous	mellifluous

1. OPALESCENT [ˌoʊpəˈles(ə)nt] *adj.* iridescent like an opal   **rhyming sound –ent**

       The beautiful girl turned her **opalescent** eyes on him.

       Word Families: **opal** *n.*; **opalescence** *n.*

2. ferment   ['fɜr‚ment] *n.* commotion; unrest; *v.* undergo fermentation

       The whole country has been in a state of political **ferment** for some months.

       Word Families: **fermentation** *n.*; **fermentable** *adj.*

3. fervent   ['fɜrv(ə)nt] *adj.* very enthusiastic and sincere about something

       Their claims have been **fervently** denied by the committee.

       Word Families: **fervency** *n.*; **fervently** *adv.*

4. putrescent [pju'tresənt] *adj.* decaying and smelling unpleasant

Some social reformers believe that the capitalist system is definitely **putrescent** and dying.

Word Families: **putrescence** *n.;* **putrescently** *adv.*

5. adolescent [ˌædə'les(ə)nt] *n. adj.* (person) between puberty and adulthood

An **adolescent** is often caught up in fantastic thoughts.

Word Families: **adolescents** *n.pl;* **adolescence** *n.*

6. OPPROBRIOUS [ə'probriəs] *adj.* deserving to be criticized severely for wrong one has

done   **rhyming sound -ous**

He ransacked an extensive vocabulary in order to find **opprobrious**

names to call her.

7. captious ['kæpʃəs] *adj.* intending to find fault and make criticism

His criticism was always **captious** and frivolous, never offering

constructive suggestions.

Word Families: **captiousness** *n.;* **captiously** *adv.*

8. horrendous [hə'rendəs] *adj.* extremely bad or shocking

She described her trip as the most **horrendous** experience of her life.

Word Families: **horrendously** *adv.*

9. lecherous ['letʃərəs] *adj.* (of a man) having or showing excessive sexual desire

Mary felt that she could never avoid the **lecherous** eyes of her boss;
therefore, she quit her office job.

Word Families: **lecherousness** *n.;* **lecherously** *adv.*

10. mellifluous [mə'lɪfluəs] *adj.* pleasant to listen to

The beautiful girl's voice was distinctive, soft, and **mellifluous**.

Word Families: **mellifluousness** *n.;* **mellifluously** *adv.*

SENTENCE COMPLETION

Choose one of the new words to complete each sentence below. Make changes if necessary.

opalescent	ferment	fervent	putrescent	adolescent
opprobrious	captious	horrendous	lecherous	mellifluous

1. It is highly important that an _____ girl should be able to confide to her mother.

2. It was a debate which aroused _____ ethical arguments.

3. The young people are becoming more and more _____ about what they wear nowadays.

4. It would be pointless to repeat the details of the most _____ crimes reported.

5. The sunset was making great splashes of fiery _____ across the sky.

6. The deserted house on the top of a small hill was _____ and scary.

7. The _____ old man who handed out candies to lure girls was finally arrested.

8. He is absolutely the most _____ man I have ever seen.

9. Nevertheless, the _____ in Japanese minds grew constantly more intense.

10. Soon the apartment was filled with _____ tones.

DEFINITION MATCHING

Choose one of the new words to match each definition below.

opalescent	ferment	fervent	putrescent	adolescent
opprobrious	captious	horrendous	lecherous	mellifluous

11. (of a man) having excessive sexual desire   _____

12. pleasant to listen to   _____

13. commotion; unrest _____

14. extremely bad or shocking _____

15. deserving to be criticized severely _____

16. iridescent like an opal _____

17. tending to find fault and make criticism _____

18. very enthusiastic and sincere about something _____

19. (person) between puberty and adulthood _____

20. decaying and smelling unpleasant _____

WRITING SENTENCES

Use each new word in the box to write an original sentence.

opalescent	ferment	fervent	putrescent	adolescent
opprobrious	captious	horrendous	lecherous	mellifluous

21._____

22._____

23._____

24._____

25._____

26._____

27._____

28._____

29._____

30._____

UNIT 19

MEMORY TIPS:

Word building with Roots, Prefixes, and Suffixes:

---

ate	cause to be; as *originate, inculcate, instigate, litigate, immaculate*
con	together; as *condone*

NEW WORDS

originate	inculcate	instigate	litigate	immaculate
ozone	clone	condone	cyclone	silicone

1. ORIGINATE   [əˈrɪdʒəˌnet] *v.* to come or bring into existence   **rhyming sound –ate**

The disease **originated** in Africa at the beginning of the century.

Word Families: **origination** *n.*; **originator** *n.;* **originative** *adj.*

2. inculcate   [ˈɪnkʌlˌkeɪt] *v.* to fix an idea or belief in someone's mind

Private banks, too, are trying novel approaches to help clients **inculcate** their values in succeeding generations.

Word Families: **inculcation** *n.;* **inculcator** *n.*

3. instigate   [ˈɪnstɪˌget] *v.* to cause to happen

The congress set up a special department to **instigate** the thing.

Word Families: **instigation** *n;* **instigator** *n.*

4. litigate ['lɪtɪˌgeɪt] *v.* to ask a court of law to make a decision

Both parties agreed to settle their claim out of court rather than **litigate**.

Word Families: **litigation** *n.;* **litigator** *n*

5. immaculate [ɪˈmækjələt] *adj.* completely clean or tidy; completely flawless

His 1988 Mercedes-Benz 300 E is in **immaculate** condition.

Word Families: **immaculacy** *n.;* **immaculateness** *n.;* **immaculately** *adv.*

6. OZONE [ˈoʊˌzoʊn] *n.* strong-smelling form of oxygen **rhyming sound -one**

The **ozone** layer blocks some harmful rays which the sun gives off.

Word Families: **ozonic** *adj.*

7. clone [kloʊn] *n.* animal or plant produced artificially from the cells of another animal or plant; an exact copy of an animal or plant

A team of scientists from the Great Britain were the first to successfully **clone** an animal.

Word Families: **clonal** *adj.*

8. condone [kənˈdoʊn] *v.* to overlook or forgive (wrongdoing)

Terrorism can never be **condoned**.

Word Families: **condonation** *n.;* **condoner** *n.*

9. cyclone [ˈsaɪˌkloʊn] *n.* a severe storm in which the winds spins in a circle

A **cyclone** in the Bay of Bengal is threatening the eastern Indian states.

Word Families: **cyclonic** *adj.;* **cyclonically** *adv.*

10. silicone [ˈsɪlɪˌkoʊn] *n.* substance made from silicon and used in lubricants or paints

NIH scientists were asked by Congress to study the safety of **silicone** breast implants.

Word Families: **silicon** *n.*

SENTENCE COMPLETION

Choose one of the new words to complete each sentence below. Make changes if necessary.

originate	inculcate	instigate	litigate	immaculate
ozone	clone	condone	cyclone	silicone

1. Did the council ever authorize the creation of a _____ army?

2. While many in China are fond of American culture, any attempt to _____ Chinese people with American values can be risky.

3. We can never _____ what he has done to the community.

4. As always, Michael was _____ dressed.

5. The _____ has resulted in the death of thousands of people.

6. It would not be worthwhile to _____ a nuclear attack.

7. What they find could provide clues to what might happen worldwide if _____ depletion continues.

8. Many species, for example, _____ in small populations.

9. A _____ filled version is available as an option for service at measuring points subject to strong vibration.

10. By contrast, the SEC is widely viewed as more prone to _____.

DEFINITION MATCHING

Choose one of the new words to match each definition below.

originate	inculcate	instigate	litigate	immaculate
ozone	clone	condone	cyclone	silicone

11. completely flawless _____

12. a storm in which the winds spins in a circle _____

13. to fix an idea or belief in someone's mind _____

14. substance made from silicon _____

15. to overlook or forgive (wrongdoing) _____

16. to come or bring into existence _____

17. an exact copy of an animal or plant _____

18. to ask a court of law to make a decision _____

19. strong-smelling form of oxygen _____

20. to cause to happen _____

WRITING SENTENCES

Use each new word in the box to write an original sentence.

originate	inculcate	instigate	litigate	immaculate
ozone	clone	condone	cyclone	silicone

21. _____

22. _____

23. _____

24. _____

25. _____

26. _____

27. _____

28. _____

29. _____

30. _____

UNIT 20

MEMORY TIPS:

Word building with Roots, Prefixes, and Suffixes:

---

able	able; as *palpable, viable, tractable, immutable, irreparable*
equi	equal; as *equinox*
im, ir	not; as *immutable, irreparable*
ortho	straight; as *orthodox*

NEW WORDS

palpable	viable	tractable	immutable	irreparable
paradox	jukebox	smallpox	equinox	orthodox

1. PALPABLE ['pælpəb(ə)l] *adj.* obvious or very easily noticed **rhyming sound –able**

There is a **palpable** difference in their ages.

Word Families: **palpability** *n.;* **palpably** *adv.*

2. viable ['vaɪəb(ə)l] *adj.* able to be done, or worth doing

Cash alone will not make Eastern Europe's banks **viable**.

Word Families: **viability** *n.;* **viably** *adv.*

3. tractable ['træktəb(ə)l] *adj.* easy to deal with

The country's least **tractable** social problems are unemployment and crimes.

Word Families: **tractability** *n.;* **tractably** *adv.*

4. immutable   [ɪ'mjutəb(ə)l] *adj.* impossible to change

There are no eternal and **immutable** principles of right and wrong.

Word Families: **immutability** *n.;* **immutably** *adv.*

5. irreparable   [ɪ'rep(ə)rəb(ə)l] *adj.* extremely bad and cannot be repaired

The storm did **irreparable** damage to the small mountain village.

Word Families: **irreparability** *n.;* **irreparably** *adj.*

6. PARADOX   ['perə,dɑks] *n.* statement that seems self-contradictory but may be true
rhyming sound -ox

The **paradox** is that the region's most dynamic economies have the

most primitive financial systems.

Word Families: **paradoxes** *n.pl.*

7. jukebox   ['dʒuk,bɑks] *n.* coin operated machine that plays music

She got up, put some money in the **jukebox**, then sat back down

Word Families: **jukeboxes** *n.pl.*

8. smallpox   ['smɔl,pɑks] *n.* contagious disease with blisters that leave scars

In 1742 he suffered a fatal attack of **smallpox**.

9. equinox   ['ekwɪ,nɑks] *n.* time of year when day and night are of equal length

The Autumnal **Equinox** is the best time for wheat-sowing.

Word Families: **equinoxes** *n.pl.*

10. orthodox   ['ɔrθə,dɑks] *adj.* conforming to established views

These people are predominantly Russian **Orthodox** by religion.

Word Families: **orthodoxly** *adv.*

SENTENCE COMPLETION

Choose one of the new words to complete each sentence below. Make changes if necessary.

palpable	viable	tractable	immutable	irreparable
paradox	jukebox	smallpox	equinox	orthodox

1. The Nixon Administration deliberately withhold supplies from Israel to make it more _____ in negotiations.

2. The other point of intersection of equator and the ecliptic is called the Autumnal _____.

3. Flattery in its most _____ form had lost its force with her.

4. A new outbreak of _____ occurred in 1928.

5. His ideas about love and marriage are very _____.

6. The _____ ground out an incessant stream of pop music.

7. Our nature is not considered _____, either socially or biologically.

8. He has just made an _____ mistake.

9. Death itself is a _____, the end yet the beginning.

10. It is only their investment that makes the program economically _____.

DEFINITION MATCHING

Choose one of the new words to match each definition below.

palpable	viable	tractable	immutable	irreparable
paradox	jukebox	smallpox	equinox	orthodox

11. time of year day and night are the same length _____

12. conforming to established views _____

13. easy to deal with   _____

14. contagious disease with blisters that leave scars   _____

15. coin operated machine that plays music   _____

16. obvious or very easily noticed   _____

17. statement that seems self-contradictory   _____

18. extremely bad and cannot be repaired   _____

19. able to be done, or worth doing   _____

20. impossible to change   _____

WRITING SENTENCES

Use each new word in the box to write an original sentence.

palpable	viable	tractable	immutable	irreparable
paradox	jukebox	smallpox	equinox	orthodox

21._____

22._____

23._____

24._____

25._____

26._____

27._____

28._____

29._____

30._____

UNIT 21

MEMORY TIPS:

Word building with Roots, Prefixes, and Suffixes:

---

de	down, from; as *depravity*
dis	apart, away; as *disparity*
ity	state or quality; as *parity, brevity, alacrity, depravity, disparity*
morph	shape; as *amorphous*
ous	full of; as *parsimonious, arduous, amorphous, ambiguous, anonymous*

NEW WORDS

parity	brevity	alacrity	depravity	disparity
parsimonious	arduous	amorphous	ambiguous	anonymous

1. PARITY   ['perəti] *n.* equality or equivalence   **rhyming sound –ity**

Women have yet to achieve wage or occupational **parity** in many fields.

Word Families: **parities** *n. pl.*

2. brevity   ['brevəti] *n.* the use of a few words; the fact that something only lasts a short time

The **brevity** of the concert disappointed most of the audience.

3. alacrity   [ə'lækrəti] *n.* promptness, speed, or eagerness

Although the man was very old, he still moved with **alacrity**.

4. depravity   [dɪˈprævəti] *n.* behavior that is immoral or evil

The patterns of human history mix decency and **depravity** in equal measure.

5. disparity   [dɪˈsperəti] *n.* a difference between things

The wide **disparity** between the rich and the poor is obvious in this country.

Word Families: **disparities** *n.pl.*

6. PARSIMONIOUS [ˈbɔɪst(ə)rəs] *adj.* not willing to give or spend money   **rhyming sound -ious**

At home, the man was churlish, **parsimonious,** and cruel to his daughter.

Word Families: **parsimoniousness** *n.;* **parsimoniously** *adv.*

7. arduous   [ˈɑrdjuəs] *adj.* extremely difficult and involving a lot of effort

The task was more **arduous** than he had imagined.

Word Families: **arduousness** *n.;* **arduously** *adv.*

8. amorphous   [əˈmɔrfəs] *adj.* with no clear shape, design, or structure

No one could really understand his **amorphous** ideas.

Word Families: **amorphousness** *n.;* **amorphously** *adv.*

9. ambiguous   [æmˈbɪgjuəs] *adj.* confusing or not definite

The Foreign Minister's remarks clarify an **ambiguous** statement issued earlier this week.

Word Families: **ambiguousness** *n;* **ambiguously** *adv.*

10. anonymous   [əˈnɑnɪməs] *adj.* by someone whose name is unknown or withheld

You can remain **anonymous** if you wish in this matter.

Word Families: **anonymity** *n.;* **anonymously** *adv.*

SENTENCE COMPLETION

Choose one of the new words to complete each sentence below. Make changes if necessary.

parity	brevity	alacrity	depravity	disparity
parsimonious	arduous	amorphous	ambiguous	anonymous

1. The great _____ between the teams did not make for an entertaining game.

2. It is an _____ colorless or white powder.

3. Some of the codes are not shown for the purpose of _____.

4. Her claim was attended to with _____ by the insurance company.

5. The refugees made an _____ journey through the mountains.

6. The evil man led a life of total _____.

7. The government was ready to let the pound sink to _____ with the dollar if necessary.

8. We have received three _____ letters from Palestine to date, in addition to one suspicious package.

9. The wording in the agreement is so _____ that it leads to misinterpretations.

10. The millionaire's _____ nature did not permit him to enjoy any luxuries.

DEFINITION MATCHING

Choose one of the new words to match each definition below.

parity	brevity	alacrity	depravity	disparity
parsimonious	arduous	amorphous	ambiguous	anonymous

11. confusing or not definite _____

12. by someone whose name is unknown _____

13. extremely difficult and involving a lot of effort _____

14. promptness, speed, or eagerness _____

15. with no clear shape, design, or structure   _____

16. equality or equivalence   _____

17. not willing to give or spend money   _____

18. behavior that is immoral or evil   _____

19. the use of a few words   _____

20. a difference between things   _____

WRITING SENTENCES

Use each new word in the box to write an original sentence.

parity	brevity	alacrity	depravity	disparity
parsimonious	arduous	amorphous	ambiguous	anonymous

21. _____

22. _____

23. _____

24. _____

25. _____

26. _____

27. _____

28. _____

29. _____

30. _____

UNIT 22

MEMORY TIPS:

Word building with Roots, Prefixes, and Suffixes:

im	non; as *impunity*
ity	state or quality; as *paucity, probity, frugality, humility, impunity*
pro	forward, before; as *probity*

NEW WORDS

paucity	probity	frugality	humility	impunity
penury	fury	jury	mercury	perjury

1. PAUCITY ['pɔsəti] *n.* a small amount of something that is not enough **rhyming sound –ity**

The **paucity** of fruit in this region was caused by the drought.

2. probity ['proʊbəti] *n.* a very moral and honest way of behaving

A judge must be a person of unquestioned **probity**.

3. frugality [fruˈgælətɪ] *n.* being thrifty and meager

Certainly, we must not allow this **frugality** to cause a depression.

Word Families: **frugal** *adj.*; **frugally** *adv.*

4. humility [hjuˈmɪləti] *n.* quality of being humble

Humility is a key virtue in a leader, too.

5. impunity   [ɪmˈpjunəti] *n.* without punishment

Mr. Cook said future aggressors would be able to act with impunity if the objectives of the UN weren't met.

6. PENURY   [ˈpenjʊri] *n.* the state of being extremely poor   **rhyming sound -icious**

Hardship and **penury** wore him out before his time.

7. fury   [ˈfjʊri] *n.* a feeling of very strong anger

The innocent girl screamed and her face was distorted with **fury** and pain.

Word Families: **furies** *n.pl;* **furious** *adj.;* **furiously** *adv.*

8. jury   [ˈdʒʊri] *n.* group of people sworn to deliver a verdict in a court of law

The **jury** found him guilty of manslaughter.

Word Families: **juries** *n.pl.*

9. mercury   [ˈmɜrkjəri] *n.* silver liquid metal; **Mercury**, the planet near the sun

The liquid we can see in thermometers is **mercury**.

10. perjury   [ˈpɜrdʒəri] *n.* the crime of lying when you give evidence in a court of law

This witness has committed **perjury**; therefore, no reliance can be placed on her evidence.

Word Families: **perjuries** *n.pl;* **perjurious** *adj.*

SENTENCE COMPLETION

Choose one of the new words to complete each sentence below. Make changes if necessary.

paucity	probity	frugality	humility	impunity
penury	fury	jury	mercury	perjury

1. No one can commit crimes with _____.

2. However, there is a _____ of research on the issue with Japanese subjects.

3. The _____ has not reached a verdict yet.

4. She felt that a wave of wild _____ overcame her.

5. Michael is truly a man with a deep sense of _____.

6. This is my prayer to thee, my lord - strike, strike at the root of _____ in my heart.

7. Just as companies' financial reports are audited, businesses should create a system to ensure _____.

8. The woman was sentenced to two years in prison for committing _____.

9. By _____ the woman managed to get along on her small salary.

10. _____ is the planet closest to the Sun.

DEFINITION MATCHING

Choose one of the new words to match each definition below.

paucity	probity	frugality	humility	impunity
penury	fury	jury	mercury	perjury

11. without punishment   _____

12. silver liquid metal   _____

13. a very moral and honest way of behaving   _____

14. group of people sworn to deliver a verdict   _____

15. the crime of lying when you give evidence   _____

16. the state of being extremely poor   _____

17. a small amount of something that is not enough   _____

18. a feeling of very strong anger   _____

19. being thrifty and meager   _____

20. quality of being humble   _____

WRITING SENTENCES

Use each new word in the box to write an original sentence.

paucity	probity	frugality	humility	impunity
penury	fury	jury	mercury	perjury

21._____

22._____

23._____

24._____

25._____

26._____

27._____

28._____

29._____

30._____

UNIT 23

MEMORY TIPS:

Word building with Roots, Prefixes, and Suffixes:

---

ab	from, away; as *abnegation*
in	into, in, on; as *inventory*
ion	condition or action; as *perdition, adulation, abnegation,*
	expiration, implication

NEW WORDS

perdition	aspersion	abnegation	adulation	implication
peremptory	allegory	dilatory	inventory	perfunctory

1. PERDITION [pərˈdɪʃ(ə)n] *n.* spiritual ruin   **rhyming sound –ion**

The man trembled whenever he thought of the **perdition**.

2. aspersion   [əˈspəːʒən] *n.* the making of defamatory remarks

Carrie felt this to contain, in some way, an **aspersion** upon her ability.

3. abnegation   [ˌæbnɪˈgeʃən] *n.* the denial and rejection of a doctrine or belief

Only spontaneous love flowing with sincere generosity and self-**abnegation** can fertilize the soul of others.

4. adulation   [ˌædʒəˈleɪʃ(ə)n] *n.* great praise or admiration, especially for someone who is famous

History abounds with great men worthy of **adulation** and emulation.

5. implication   [ˌɪmplɪˈkeɪʃ(ə)n] *n.* a possible effect or result

The Attorney General was aware of the political **implication**s of his decision to prosecute the man for bribery.

Word Families: **implications** *n.pl.;* **implicational** *adj.*

6. PEREMPTORY [pəˈrempt(ə)ri] *adj.* speaking or behaving rather rudely as if you expect others to believe you immediately   **rhyming sound -ory**

In short, their position as it emerged in the three meetings with us was **peremptory** and unyielding

Word Families: **peremptoriness** *n.;* **peremptorily** *adv.*

7. allegory   [ˈæləɡəri] *n.* story with an underlying meaning as well as the literal one

"The Mysterious Stranger", his last book, is an **allegory** that suggests that life is in reality only a dream.

Word Families: **allegories** *n.pl;* **allegorist** *n.;* **allegorical** *adj.*

8. dilatory   [ˈdɪləˌtɔri] *adj.* slow to do or decide something

It is not surprising that Toyota's response has been **dilatory** and inept, because crisis management in Japan is grossly undeveloped.

Word Families: **dilatoriness** *n.;* **dilatorily** *adv.*

9. inventory   [ˈɪnvənˌtɔri] *n.* detailed list of goods and furnishings

The **inventory** showed that the store was overstocked.

Word Families: **inventories** *n.pl.*

10. perfunctory   [pərˈfʌŋkt(ə)ri] *adj.* done without much effort or interest

He made some **perfunctory** remarks at the meeting.

Word Families: **perfunctoriness** *n.;* **perfunctorily** *adv.*

SENTENCE COMPLETION

Choose one of the new words to complete each sentence below. Make changes if necessary.

perdition	aspersion	abnegation	adulation	implication
peremptory	allegory	dilatory	inventory	perfunctory

1. Such _____ has become a popular tactic in these anti-political times.

2. His authority and, by _____, that of his management team is under threat.

3. This book is a kind of _____ of Latin American history.

4. It was their remarkable spirit that had prevented them from _____.

5. His _____ tone irritated almost everybody at the meeting.

6. Her recent novel was received with _____ by critics.

7. You might expect politicians to smooth things out when civil servants are being _____.

8. In the 19th century any reference to female sexuality was considered a vile

   _____.

9. The woman could not be negative or _____ about anything.

10. This product is in compliance with the Toxic Substance Control Act's _____ requirements

DEFINITION MATCHING

Choose one of the new words to match each definition below.

perdition	aspersion	abnegation	adulation	implication
peremptory	allegory	dilatory	inventory	perfunctory

11. a possible effect or result   _____

12. detailed list of goods and furnishings   _____

13. story with both underlying and literal meaning   _____

14. done without much effort or interest _____

15. spiritual ruin _____

16. speaking or behaving rather rudely _____

17. slow to do or decide something _____

18. the denial and rejection of a doctrine or belief _____

19. great praise or admiration _____

20. the making of defamatory remarks _____

WRITING SENTENCES

Use each new word in the box to write an original sentence.

perdition	aspersion	abnegation	adulation	implication
peremptory	allegory	dilatory	inventory	perfunctory

21._____

22._____

23._____

24._____

25._____

26._____

27._____

28._____

29._____

30._____

UNIT 24

MEMORY TIPS:

Word building with Roots, Prefixes, and Suffixes:

---

ious, ous	characterized by; as *perfidious, tenuous, momentous, ominous, vociferous*
inter	between, among; as *interfuse*
per	through, intensive; as *perfidious, peruse*

NEW WORDS

perfidious	tenuous	momentous	ominous	vociferous
peruse	fuse	muse	abuse	interfuse

1. PERFIDIOUS [pər'fɪdiəs] *adj.* not able to be trusted   **rhyming sound –ous**

> This is a **perfidious** crime of aggression not only against this country but also against the freedom and independence of all nations
> *Word Families*: **perfidiousness** *n.*; **perfidiously** *adv.*

2. tenuous   ['tenjuəs] *adj.* weak and likely to change

> This decision puts the President in a somewhat **tenuous** position.

> *Word Families*: **tenuousness** *n.;* **tenuously** *adv.*

3. momentous   [moʊ'mentəs] *adj.* very important

The past five years have been among the most **momentous** in the history of science and technology.

Word Families: **momentousness** *n.;* **momentously** *adv.*

4. ominous   ['ɑmɪnəs] *adj.* threatening; indicating evil or harm

There are already **ominous** signs in the air for the industry.

Word Families: **ominousness** *n.;* **ominously** *adj.*

5. vociferous   [voʊ'sɪfərəs] *adj.* loud; shouting

A smaller programme ensures that less **vociferous** students do not get left behind.

Word Families: **vociferousness** *n.;* **vociferously** *adv..*

6. PERUSE   [pə'ruz] *v.* to read something   **rhyming sound -use**

You should **peruse** the terms and conditions carefully before using any service.

Word Families: **peruser** *n.*

7. fuse   [fjuːz] *n.* safety device for electric circuit; *v.* to join; to unite by melting

The conflict further became the **fuse** of the World War II.

Word Families: **fusion** *n.;* **fuseless** *adj.*

8. muse   [mjuz] *v.* to ponder quietly; *n.* force or person that inspires a creative artist

She once **mused** that she would have been the First Lady of the United States had she had the chance to go to college with the President.

9. abuse   [ə'bjus] *v.* to use wrongly; to ill-treat violently; *n.* wrong use; ill-treatment

"There was no **abuse**, name-calling, threats, punishment, bans or dismissals," he said.

10. interfuse   [ˌɪntə'fjuːz] *v.* to mingle, blend, or fuse thoroughly

All these mechanisms can interact and **interfuse** and form intelligently and naturally operating mechanisms.

Word Families: **interfusion** *n.*

SENTENCE COMPLETION

Choose one of the new words to complete each sentence below. Make changes if necessary.

perfidious	tenuous	momentous	ominous	vociferous
peruse	fuse	muse	abuse	interfuse

1. The second question is less _____, but more baffling.

2. He was a _____ opponent of Conservatism.

3. The cultural and historical links between the many provinces were seen to be very

   _____.

4. Anyone can _____ the details of software for whatever reason he or she likes.

5. Your _____ gossip is malicious and dangerous.

6. He spoke _____ of the world facing a war in Europe and possibly something

   greater.

7. This is the right _____ for the refrigerator.

8. The man alleged that he was verbally _____ by other soldiers.

9. We had a heated discussion on the _____ of traditional library and digital library.

10. Plenty of women have been both lover, and _____ to famous artists, like Picasso..

DEFINITION MATCHING

Choose one of the new words to match each definition below.

perfidious	tenuous	momentous	ominous	vociferous
peruse	fuse	muse	abuse	interfuse

11. force or person that inspires a creative artist   _____

12. to mingle, blend, or fuse thoroughly   _____

13. not able to be trusted   _____

14. wrong use; ill-treatment   _____

15. to join; to unite by melting   _____

16. weak and likely to change   _____

17. loud; shouting   _____

18. to read something   _____

19. threatening; indicating evil or harm   _____

20. very important   _____

WRITING SENTENCES

Use each new word in the box to write an original sentence.

perfidious	tenuous	momentous	ominous	vociferous
peruse	fuse	muse	abuse	interfuse

21. _____

22. _____

23. _____

24. _____

25. _____

26. _____

27. _____

28. _____

29. _____

30. _____

UNIT 25

MEMORY TIPS:

Word building with Roots, Prefixes, and Suffixes:

---

co	together; *as coalition*
dis	not; as *dissuasive*
ion	act of; as *petition, rendition, tuition, acquisition, coalition*
ive	relating to; as *pervasive, abrasive, dissuasive, evasive, persuasive*
pet	seek; as *petition*
per	through, intensive; as *pervasive, persuasive*

NEW WORDS

pervasive	abrasive	dissuasive	evasive	persuasive
petition	rendition	acquisition	coalition	intuition

1. PERVASIVE [pər'veɪsɪv] *adj.* spreading right through something **rhyming sound –asive**

The bigger, more **pervasive** problem is on the demand side.

Word Families: **pervasiveness** *n.;* **pervasively** *adv.*

2. abrasive [ə'breɪsɪv] *adj.* harsh and unpleasant in manner; *n.* substance for cleaning and polishing by rubbing

Jack's **abrasive** manner has won him an unenviable notoriety.

Word Families: **abrasives** *n.pl.*; **abrasiveness** *n.*

3. dissuasive   [dɪ'sweɪsɪv] *adj.* deterring somebody by persuasion from doing something

It seems that all the evidence to the contrary is not entirely **dissuasive**.

Word Families: **dissuasiveness** *n;* **dissuasion** *n.*

4. evasive   [i'veɪsɪv] *adj.* not talking or answering questions in a honest way

He was **evasive** about the details of his recent meeting with the President.

Word Families: **evasiveness** *n.;* **evasively** *adv.*

5. persuasive   [pər'sweɪsɪv] *adj.* good at making people agree to do or believe

The mayor's arguments in favor of a new school are very **persuasive**.

Word Families: **persuasiveness** *n.;* **persuasively** *adv.*

6. PETITION   [pə'tɪʃ(ə)n] *n.* formal request signed by many people; v. present a petition to
rhyming sound -ition

They recently presented the city government with a **petition** signed by 1000 people.

Word Families: **petitioner** *n.;* **petitionary** *adj.*

7. rendition   [ren'dɪʃ(ə)n] *n.* performance; translation

"He's delightful, delightful," he went on, giving the commonplace **rendition** of approval which such men know.

8. acquisition   [ˌækwɪ'zɪʃ(ə)n] *n.* thing acquired; act of getting

He devoted almost all his time to the **acquisition** of knowledge.

9. coalition   [ˌkoʊə'lɪʃ(ə)n] *n.* temporary alliance between political parties

It took five months for the **coalition** to agree on and publish a medium-term economic program.

10. intuition   [ˌɪntu'ɪʃ(ə)n] *n.* instinctive knowledge or insight without conscious reasoning

Her **intuition** was telling her that something was wrong.

Word Families: **intuitions** *n.pl..;* **intuitional** *adj.*

SENTENCE COMPLETION

Choose one of the new words to complete each sentence below. Make changes if necessary.

pervasive	abrasive	dissuasive	evasive	persuasive
petition	rendition	acquisition	coalition	intuition

1. Mary looked at the man closely to see if his _____ was intentional.

2. His _____ argument made everybody feel confused at the meeting.

3. The evidence was not really _____ enough to convince the jury.

4. Digital wireless networks are still not _____ today.

5. I had an _____ that I would find you.

6. He had been opposed by a _____ of about 50 civil rights, women's

   and Latino organizations.

7. She lifted her voice during her _____ of the classic opera song.

8. If another _____ opportunity comes up, we would certainly not rule it out.

9. Many colleagues regard Summers as _____, but Greenspan sounds affectionate.

10. His lawyers filed a _____ for all charges to be dropped.

DEFINITION MATCHING

Choose one of the new words to match each definition below.

pervasive	abrasive	dissuasive	evasive	persuasive
petition	rendition	acquisition	coalition	intuition

11. formal request signed by many people   _____

12. performance; translation   _____

13. harsh and unpleasant in manner   _____

14. thing acquired; act of getting   _____

15. instinctive knowledge   _____

16. good at making people to do or believe   _____

17. deterring somebody by persuasion from doing   _____

18. temporary alliance between political parties   _____

19. not talking or answering in a honest way   _____

20. spreading right through something   _____

WRITING SENTENCES

Use each new word in the box to write an original sentence.

pervasive	abrasive	dissuasive	evasive	persuasive
petition	rendition	acquisition	coalition	intuition

21. _____

22. _____

23. _____

24. _____

25. _____

26. _____

27. _____

28. _____

29. _____

30. _____

UNIT 26

MEMORY TIPS:

Word building with Roots, Prefixes, and Suffixes:

---

com	together; as *comprehend*
epi	upon, close to, over, after, altered; as *epistemic*
ic	of, like; as *polemic, alchemic, endemic, academic, epistemic*
port	carry, bring; as *portend*

NEW WORDS

polemic	endemic	systemic	epidemic	epistemic
portend	blend	amend	apprehend	reprehend

1. POLEMIC   [pəˈlemɪk] *n.* argument about doctrines   **rhyming sound –emic**

But underlying his **polemic** lay a disapproval of manufacturers foisting goods on consumers who did not really need them.

Word Families: **polemics** *n. pl.;* **polemicist** *n.;* **polemical** *adj.*

2. endemic   [enˈdemɪk] *adj.* very common, or strongly established in a place

Food shortages and starvation are **endemic** in certain parts of the world.

Word Families: **endemicity** *n.;* **endemism** *n.;* **endemically** *adv.*

3. systemic   [sɪˈstemɪk] *adj.* affecting all of something; affecting your whole body

The national economy is currently locked in a **systemic** crisis.

Word Families: **systemically** *adv.*

4. epidemic   [ˌepɪ'demɪk] *n.* widespread occurrence of a disease

A flu **epidemic** is sweeping through southwest region of the country.

Word Families: **epidemics** *n. pl.*

5. epistemic   [ˌɛpɪ'stimɪk] *adj.* relating to knowledge

A second version of the classical approach would focus on the **epistemic** goal of having justified or rational beliefs.

Word Families: **epistemically** *adj.*

6. PORTEND   [pɔr'tend] *n.* to be a sign or warning that something will happen   **rhyming sound -end**

The change did not **portend** a basic improvement in social conditions.

7. blend   [blend] *v.* to mix or mingle; *n.* mixture

The New City Centre offers a subtle **blend** of traditional charm with modern amenities.

8. amend   [ə'mend] *v.* to make changes to a document or law agreement

The President has agreed to **amend** the constitution and allow multi-party elections.

Word Families: **amendment** *n.;* **amender** *n.;* **amendable** *adj.*

9. apprehend   [ˌæprɪ'hend] *v.* to arrest someone; to understand something

The police have **apprehended** the killer of the old woman.

10. reprehend   [ˌrɛprɪ'hɛnd] *v.* to criticize or reprove somebody or something

His conduct deserves to be **reprehended**.

SENTENCE COMPLETION

Choose one of the new words to complete each sentence below. Make changes if necessary.

polemic	endemic	systemic	epidemic	epistemic
portend	blend	amend	apprehend	reprehend

1. Third, containing _____ financial risk is not enough to restore growth.

2. Street crime is virtually _____ in large cities in the United States.

3. Here a social communicational device is treated as a type of _____ standard.

4. Mr. Gates avoided raising the rhetorical ante with the former KGB officer, preferring instead to laugh off the _____.

5. Sometimes small events can _____ great changes.

6. The sea and sky seemed to _____ on the horizon.

7. The little mountain village was smitten by an _____.

8. The girl was severely _____ for torturing the little cat.

9. Only now can I begin to _____ the power of these forces.

10. Government has no firm position on how to _____ the two electoral methods.

DEFINITION MATCHING

Choose one of the new words to match each definition below.

polemic	endemic	systemic	epidemic	epistemic
portend	blend	amend	apprehend	reprehend

11. to arrest someone   _____

12. to criticize or reprove somebody or something   _____

13. argument about doctrines   _____

14. to make changes to a document or agreement   _____

15. to mix or mingle   _____

16. very common, or strongly established in a place _____

17. to be a sign that something will happen _____

18. widespread occurrence of a disease _____

19. relating to knowledge _____

20. affecting all of something _____

WRITING SENTENCES

Use each new word in the box to write an original sentence.

polemic	endemic	systemic	epidemic	epistemic
portend	blend	amend	apprehend	reprehend

21._____

22._____

23._____

24._____

25._____

26._____

27._____

28._____

29._____

30._____

UNIT 27

MEMORY TIPS:

Word building with Roots, Prefixes, and Suffixes:

---

con	together; as *concept*
in	not; as *inept*
ious	characterized by; as *precocious, spacious, specious, atrocious, ferocious*
inter	between, among; as *intercept*

NEW WORDS

precept	concept	incept	inept	intercept
precocious	spacious	specious	atrocious	ferocious

1. PRECEPT ['pri,sept] *n.* rule of behavior **rhyming sound –ept**

Armed with certain **precepts**, a number of doctors may slip into deceptive practices.

Word Families: **precepts** *n. pl.;* **perceptive** *adj.*

2. concept ['kɒnsept] *n.* abstract or general idea

She added that the **concept** of arranged marriages is misunderstood in the west.

Word Families: **concepts** *n.pl.*

3. incept [ɪn'sept] *v.*. to begin; to start something

The training program has been successful since its **inception**.

Word Families: **inception** *n. pl.;* **inceptor** *n.*

4. inept [ɪ'nept] *n.* clumsy; lacking skill

Generally speaking, David Campbell was an **inept** politician.

Word Families: **ineptitude** *n;* **ineptness** *n.;* **ineptly** *adv.*.

5. intercept [,ɪntər'sept] *v.* to stop, catch or take control of somebody or something

The small country plans to **intercept** foreign missiles when it is necessary.

Word Families: **interception** *n.;* **interceptive** *adj.*

6. PRECOCIOUS [prɪ'koʊʃəs] *adj.* having developed or matured too early or too soon
   rhyming sound -icious

Despite her **precocious** talent for mathematics, she failed it at the graduation test.

Word Families: **precociousness** *n.;* **precocity** *n.;* **precociously** *adv.*

7. spacious ['speɪʃəs] *adj.* having a large capacity or area

They have moved to a more **spacious** residence on the west side of Vancouver.

Word Families: **spaciousness** *n.;* **spaciously** *adv.*

8. specious ['spiʃəs] *adj.* seeming to be true but in fact wrong

An international regulator is better positioned to resist these often **specious** arguments.

9. atrocious [ə'troʊʃəs] *adj.* very evil or cruel; very unpleasant

The judge said he the man had committed **atrocious** crimes against women.

Word Families: **atrociousness** *n;* **atrociously** *adv.*.

10. ferocious [fə'roʊʃəs] *adj.* savagely fierce or cruel

Mr. Obama can also fairly complain that he has faced **ferocious** opposition.

Word Families: **ferociousness** *n.;* **ferociously** *adv.*

SENTENCE COMPLETION

Choose one of the new words to complete each sentence below. Make changes if necessary.

precept	concept	incept	inept	intercept
precocious	spacious	specious	atrocious	ferocious

1. A high ceiling creates a feeling of _____.

2. It is unlikely that the President was convinced by such _____ arguments.

3. Since its _____ in 1975, our export business has enjoyed tremendous growth.

4. He felt confronted by the most _____ suffering he had ever known.

5. Freud first mentioned this _____ in his paper "On Narcissism".

6. Many of her letters were _____ by the Secret Service.

7. It occurs to me that example is always more efficacious than _____.

8. She was _____ and lacked the skills to govern such an international organization.

9. The police had to deal with some of the most _____ violence in the city.

10. Thirty years later, this _____ youth was to be the first President of the United States.

DEFINITION MATCHING

Choose one of the new words to match each definition below.

precept	concept	incept	inept	intercept
precocious	spacious	specious	atrocious	ferocious

11. having developed or matured too early   _____

12. seeming to be true but in fact wrong   _____

13. rule of behavior   _____

14. stop or catch somebody or something   _____

15. savagely fierce or cruel   _____

16. abstract or general idea   _____

17. very evil or cruel; very unpleasant   _____

18. having a large capacity or area   _____

19. to begin; to start something   _____

20. clumsy; lacking skill   _____

WRITING SENTENCES

Use each new word in the box to write an original sentence.

precept	concept	incept	inept	intercept
precocious	spacious	specious	atrocious	ferocious

21._____

22._____

23._____

24._____

25._____

26._____

27._____

28._____

29._____

30._____

UNIT 28

MEMORY TIPS:

Word building with Roots, Prefixes, and Suffixes:

---

ate	Verb: cause to be; as *preponderate, prate, profligate, elaborate, repudiate*
con	together; as *consolidate, conservative*
extra	out of, beyond; as *extrapolate*
ive	relating to; as *prerogative, correlative, derivative, figurative, preservative*
pre	before; as *preservative*

NEW WORDS

preponderate	prate	profligate	elaborate	repudiate
prerogative	correlative	derivative	figurative	preservative

1. PREPONDERATE [prɪˈpɑndəˌret] *v.* to be greater in force, amount or influence **rhyming sound –ate**

Therefore, shaping about innovation psychology should not **preponderate** over the principle with practice determining theory.

Word Families: **preponderance** *n.*

2. prate [preɪt] *v.* to talk in a silly way for a long time; to babble

I know the age better than you do, though you will **prate** about it so tediously.

3. profligate   ['prɑflɪgɪt] *adj.* wasteful

The young millionaire's **profligate** lifestyle resulted in bankruptcy.

Word Families: **profligacy** *n.;* **profligately** *adj.*

4. elaborate   [ɪ'læb(ə)rət] *v.* to give more details about something; *n.* very detailed and complicated

Elaborate efforts at the highest level have been made to conceal the problem.

Word Families: **elaboration** *n.;* **elaborately** *adj.*

5. repudiate   [rɪ'pjudiˌeɪt] *v.* to say formally that something is not true

The Prime Minister has **repudiated** racist remarks made by a member of the Conservative Party.

6. PREROGATIVE [prɪ'rɑgətɪv] *n.* privilege or right   **rhyming sound -ative**

This **prerogative** is left to the 1,000 or more authorized business schools spread throughout the country.

Word Families: **prerogatives** *n.pl.*

7. correlative   [kə'relətɪv] *adj.* being placed in a mutual relationship

Time is **correlative** with speed.

Word Families: **correlativity** *n.;* **correlation** *n.; re* **correlatively** *adv.*

8. derivative   [dɪ'rɪvətɪv] *adj.* words, idea, etc. derived from another; *n.* something that has developed from something else

This isn't an entirely new car, but a new **derivative** of the Citroen XM.

9. figurative   ['fɪgərətɪv] *adj.* (of language) abstract, imaginative, or symbolic

Europe, with Germany literally and **figuratively** at its centre, is still at the start of a remarkable transformation.

10. preservative [prɪ'zɜrvətɪv] *n.* chemical that prevents decay

Salt is a **preservative** for meat or fish.

SENTENCE COMPLETION

Choose one of the new words to complete each sentence below. Make changes if necessary.

preponderate	prate	profligate	elaborate	repudiate
prerogative	correlative	derivative	figurative	preservative

1. Similarly Americans have been _____ in the handling of mineral resources.

2. However, the Citizens opinion does not necessarily _____ that proposition.

3. His task was to _____ policies which would make a market economy compatible with a clean environment

4. Ethnic Chinese _____ in the population of Singapore.

5. Making such decisions is not the sole _____ of managers.

6. If the hen does not _____, she will not lay.

7. This kind of wood is treated with _____ to prevent decay.

8. A lot of what you see in stand-up comedy today is very _____.

9. No one was doing realistic _____ art other than cowboys and Indians.

10. The price includes the _____ fees to exporting all the cargos.

DEFINITION MATCHING

Choose one of the new words to match each definition below.

preponderate	prate	profligate	elaborate	repudiate
prerogative	correlative	derivative	figurative	preservative

11. wasteful   _____

12. privilege or right   _____

13. to be greater in force, amount or influence _____

14. chemical that prevents decay _____

15. (of language) abstract, imaginative, or symbolic _____

16. to talk in a silly way for a long time _____

17. words, idea, etc. derived from another _____

18. to say formally that something is wrong _____

19. being placed in a mutual relationship _____

20. to give more details about something _____

WRITING SENTENCES

Use each new word in the box to write an original sentence.

preponderate	prate	profligate	elaborate	repudiate
prerogative	correlative	derivative	figurative	preservative

21. _____

22. _____

23. _____

24. _____

25. _____

26. _____

27. _____

28. _____

29. _____

30. _____

UNIT 29

MEMORY TIPS:

Word building with Roots, Prefixes, and Suffixes:

---

dia	across, through; as *diagnosis*
ic	of, like; as *prolific, horrific, specific, terrific, colorific*
pro	before; as *prognosis, prolific*

NEW WORDS

prognosis	hypnosis	diagnosis	scoliosis	tuberculosis
prolific	horrific	specific	terrific	colorific

1. PROGNOSIS [prɑgˈnoʊsɪs] *n.* doctor's forecast about an illness; any forecast **rhyming sound –osis**

The doctor's **prognosis** was that Laurence might walk within 12 months.

Word Families: **prognoses** *n. pl.*

2. hypnosis [hɪpˈnoʊsɪs] *n.* artificially induced state of relaxation in which the mind is more than usually receptive to suggestion

This is the **hypnosis** technique which can help self-healing.

Word Families: **hypnoses** *n. pl.;* **hypnotic** *adj.;* **hypnotically** *adv.*

3. diagnosis [ˌdaɪəgˈnoʊsɪs] *n.* a statement about what disease someone has

The doctor made his **diagnosis** after studying the patient's symptoms.

Word Families: **diagnoses** *n. pl.;* **diagnostic** *adj.*

4. scoliosis   [ˌskoʊlɪˈoʊsɪs] *n.* an excessive sideways curvature of the human spine

Progression of **scoliosis** can occur in patients who experience rapid growth.

Word Families: **scoliotic** *adj.*

5. tuberculosis   [tʊˌbɜrkjəˈloʊsɪs] *n.* a serious infectious disease affecting your lungs

HIV infection reduces the body immunity against mycobacterium **tuberculosis**.

6. PROLIFIC   [prəˈlɪfɪk] *adj.* productive; fertile   **rhyming sound -ific**

Mice are **prolific** breeders.

Word Families: **prolificacy** *n.;* **prolificness** *n.;* **prolifically** *adv.*

7. horrific   [həˈrɪfɪk] *adj.* so shocking that upsets you

President Obama also called it a "**horrific** and cowardly attack."

Word Families: **horrifically** *adv.*

8. specific   [spəˈsɪfɪk] *adj.* exact and detailed

He would not discuss whether any **specific** regulatory demands might be deal-breakers.

Word Families: **specificity** *n.;* **specificness** *n.;* **specifically** *adv.*

9. terrific   [təˈrɪfɪk] *adj.* very good or interesting

The company tried to tell customers they were still getting a "**terrific** value."

Word Families: **terrifically** *adv.*

10. colorific   [ˌkʌləˈrɪfɪk] *adj.* producing or giving color to something

We should pay special attention to the **colorific** configuration of the bathroom due to its limited space.

SENTENCE COMPLETION

Choose one of the new words to complete each sentence below. Make changes if necessary.

prognosis	hypnosis	diagnosis	scoliosis	tuberculosis
prolific	horrific	specific	terrific	colorific

1. The plain radiograph of the spine demonstrated mild _____.

2. Mary Jones is a _____ writer of children's stories.

3. The _____ for the economy is uncertain.

4. The error message is not _____, but at least you know where it is.

5. The film showed the most _____ murder scenes we had ever seen.

6. _____ was deferred pending further assessment.

7. All of a sudden there was a _____ bang and a flash of smoke.

8. The _____ features reflect the local culture from historic evolvement, ethical mentality, religion, etc.

9. Some people claim that they have been cured of smoking by _____.

10. _____ is a curable disease.

DEFINITION MATCHING

Choose one of the new words to match each definition below.

prognosis	hypnosis	diagnosis	scoliosis	tuberculosis
prolific	horrific	specific	terrific	colorific

11. a serious infectious disease affecting your lungs _____

12. so shocking that upsets you _____

13. producing or giving color to something _____

14. a sideways curvature of the human spine _____

15. very good or interesting _____

16. artificially induced state of relaxation _____

17. exact and detailed _____

18. a statement about what disease someone has _____

19. productive; fertile _____

20. doctor's forecast of an illness; any forecast _____

WRITING SENTENCES

Use each new word in the box to write an original sentence.

prognosis	hypnosis	diagnosis	scoliosis	tuberculosis
prolific	horrific	specific	terrific	colorific

21. _____

22. _____

23. _____

24. _____

25. _____

26. _____

27. _____

28. _____

29. _____

30. _____

UNIT 30

MEMORY TIPS:

Word building with Roots, Prefixes, and Suffixes:

---

ate	Verb: cause to be; as *prognosticate, implicate, eradicate, reiterate, relegate, propitiate, deviate, initiate, mediate, differentiate*
in	in, into, on; as *implicate*
re	back, again; as *reiterate, relegate*

NEW WORDS

prognosticate	implicate	reiterate	relegate	eradicate
propitiate	deviate	initiate	mediate	differentiate

1. PROGNOSTICATE [prɑgˈnɑstɪˌket] *v.* to make a prediction about; to tell in advance
rhyming sound –ate

It has long been fashionable for visionaries to **prognosticate** about the direction technology.

Word Families: **prognosticator** *n.;* **prognosticatory** *adj.*

2. implicate [ˈɪmplɪˌkeɪt] *v.* to indicate indirectly; to suggest something

His investigation would eventually **implicate** his brother in the crime.

Word Families: **implication** *n.;* **implicatively** *adv.*

3. reiterate   [ri'ɪtə,reɪt] *v.* to repeat something in order to emphasize it

The Government deems it necessary to **reiterate** its position and policy on the these matters.

4. relegate   ['relə,geɪt] *v.* to banish; to assign to a inferior position

Some scientists **relegate** parapsychology to the sphere of quackery.

5. eradicate   [ɪ'rædɪ,keɪt] *v.* to get rid of something completely

Although these substances would not **eradicate** the AIDS virus, still they can effectively control their reproduction.

6. PROPITIATE [proʊ'pɪʃi,eɪt] *v.* to appease; to win the favor of   **rhyming sound -iate**

McKinley was eager to **propitiate** the agrarian Middle West after his close victory over Bryan in 1896.

Word Families: **propitiator** *n.;* **propitiatory** *adj.*

7. deviate   ['divi,eɪt] *v.* to depart from one's previous behavior; to differ from others in thoughts or beliefs

His statement seemed slightly to **deviate** from the truth.

8. initiate   [ɪ'nɪʃi,eɪt] *v.* to begin

The military preparations that have occurred do not indicate that any party intends to **initiate** hostilities.

Word Families: **initiation** *n.;* **initiatory** *adj.*

9. mediate   ['midi,eɪt] *v.* to try to end a disagreement between two parties

They may be able to **mediate** between parties with different interests.

Word Families: **mediation** *n;* **mediator** *n.;* **mediatory** *adj.*

10. differentiate   [,dɪfə'rɛnʃi,et] *v.* to mark as different

A child may not be able to **differentiate** between his imagination and the real world.

Word Families: **differentiation** *n.;* **differentiator** *n.*

SENTENCE COMPLETION

Choose one of the new words to complete each sentence below. Make changes if necessary.

prognosticate	implicate	reiterate	relegate	eradicate
propitiate	deviate	initiate	mediate	differentiate

1. We can no longer _____ Afghanistan to the bottom of our priority list.

2. From very early on he believed a military revolution was necessary and he has never _____ from that ideological path.

3. We must take this good opportunity to fight an excellent _____ battle.

4. It would be very hard to _____ about the company's earnings next year.

5. At this stage the little baby cannot _____ one person from another.

6. Our trip was _____ by the manager of the community centre.

7. These scandals _____ many of the country's most powerful leaders.

8. The ceremony was believed to encourage fertility, demonstrate piety, and _____ the gods.

9. His wife had a fight with his mother; he tried every means to _____ between them.

10. I continue to _____ that students are expected to be respectful when learning at school.

DEFINITION MATCHING

Choose one of the new words to match each definition below.

prognosticate	implicate	reiterate	relegate	eradicate
propitiate	deviate	initiate	mediate	differentiate

11. to get rid of something completely _____

12. to mark as different _____

13. to appease; to win the favor of _____

14. to try to end a disagreement between two parties _____

15. to begin _____

16. to make a prediction about _____

17. to repeat _____

18. to differ from others in thoughts or beliefs _____

19. to indicate indirectly _____

20. to banish; to assign to a inferior position _____

WRITING SENTENCES

Use each new word in the box to write an original sentence.

prognosticate	implicate	reiterate	relegate	eradicate
propitiate	deviate	initiate	mediate	differentiate

21. _____

22. _____

23. _____

24. _____

25. _____

26. _____

27. _____

28. _____

29. _____

30. _____

UNIT 31

MEMORY TIPS:

Word building with Roots, Prefixes, and Suffixes:

---

cid	cut, kill; as *incident*
co	together; as *coincident*
in	in, into, on; as *incident*
pro	before; as *protocol, provident*

NEW WORDS

protocol	menthol	alcohol	parasol	cholesterol
provident	diffident	evident	incident	coincident

1. PROTOCOL ['proʊtəˌkɔl] *n.* rules of behavior for formal occasions **rhyming sound –ol**

Climate change negotiators are trying to come up with a workable draft document to replace the 1997 Kyoto **Protocol**.

Word Families: **protocols** *n. pl.*

2. menthol ['menˌθɑl] *n.* a substance that smells and tastes like mint

Menthol cigarettes are almost produced entirely in the US.

3. alcohol ['ælkəˌhɔl] *n.* intoxicating drinks generally

Thomas has finally got rid of his addiction to **alcohol**.

Word Families: **alcoholic** *adj.*

4. parasol ['pærə,sɔl] *n.* umbrella-like sunshade

She smiled beneath the **parasol** at the soft warmth of the day.

Word Families: **parasols** *n. pl.*

5. cholesterol [kə'lestərɑl] *n.* fatty substance found in animal tissue, an excess of which can cause heart disease

Eating garlic can significantly reduce **cholesterol** in the blood.

6. PROVIDENT ['prɑvɪdənt] *adj.* thrifty; showing foresight   **rhyming sound -icious**

The housing **provident** fund system needs to be reformed immediately to meet the needs of the buyers.

Word Families: **providence** *n.;* **providently** *adv.*

7. diffident ['dɪfɪdənt] *adj.* shy

The beautiful girl has a politely **diffident** manner.

Word Families: **diffidence** *n.;* **diffidently** *adv.*

8. evident ['evɪdənt] *adj.* easy to see, notice, or understand

The spokesman made it **evident** that no compromise was yet in sight.

Word Families: **evidence** *n.;* **evidently** *adv.*

9. incident ['ɪnsɪdənt] *n.* something that happens; event involving violence

In a statement, the President Bush said he 'was shocked and deeply saddened' by the **incident**.

Word Families: **incidents** *n.pl.*

10. coincident [ko'ɪnsɪdənt] *adj.* in agreement

The results were **coincident** with the calculated data and the thermocouple measurements.

Word Families: **coincidence** *n.;* **coincidently** *adv.*

SENTENCE COMPLETION

Choose one of the new words to complete each sentence below. Make changes if necessary.

protocol	menthol	alcohol	parasol	cholesterol
provident	diffident	evident	incident	coincident

1. They are determining the serum-protein and _____ levels.

2. He felt a little _____ about asking concerning her success.

3. The truth was by no means _____ when Galileo first suggested it.

4. _____ is often a very potent trigger for cluster headache, as well.

5. We must observe the correct _____ in business.

6. The police said that the attack was an isolated _____.

7. Mary has been _____ ever since she was a little girl.

8. The _____ in the toothpaste gives a cooling sensation.

9. The results of model experiments are well _____ with those of finite element method.

10. All kinds of umbrellas include stick, folder, beach, golf and _____.

DEFINITION MATCHING

Choose one of the new words to match each definition below.

protocol	menthol	alcohol	parasol	cholesterol
provident	diffident	evident	incident	coincident

11. in agreement   _____

12. umbrella-like sunshade   _____

13. fatty substance found in animal tissue   _____

14. event involving violence   _____

15. easy to see, notice, or understand   _____

16. rules of behavior for formal occasions   _____

17. thrifty; showing foresight   _____

18. shy   _____

19. a substance that smells and tastes like mint   _____

20. intoxicating drinks generally   _____

WRITING SENTENCES

Use each new word in the box to write an original sentence.

protocol	menthol	alcohol	parasol	cholesterol
provident	diffident	evident	incident	coincident

21._____

22._____

23._____

24._____

25._____

26._____

27._____

28._____

29._____

30._____

UNIT 32

MEMORY TIPS:

Word building with Roots, Prefixes, and Suffixes:

---

ad	to; as *adjoin*
dis	apart, not; as *disjoin*
ex	out of, from; as *exile*
ile	capable of being; as *puerile, agile, docile, futile*

NEW WORDS

puerile	agile	docile	exile	futile
purloin	adjoin	conjoin	disjoin	rejoin

1. PUERILE ['pjʊrəl] *adj.* silly and childish **rhyming sound –ile**

His **puerile** pranks sometimes offended his more mature friends.

Word Families: **puerility** *n.;* **puerilely** *adv.*

2. agile ['æ,dʒəl] *adj.* able to move quickly and easily

His intellect and mental **agility** have never been in doubt.

Word Families: **agility** *n;* **agilely** *adv.*

3. docile ['dɒsɪl] *adj.* (of a person or animal) easily controlled

The soldiers were grateful and **docile**, made almost childlike by their wounds.

Word Families: **docility** *n.;* **docilely** *adv.*

4. futile   ['fjut(ə)l] *adj.* unsuccessful, or useless

Without microscopes and other modern equipment, attempts to teach science were **futile**.

Word Families: **futility** *n.;* **futilely** *adv.*

5. revile   [rɪ'vaɪl] *v.* to hate and criticize someone or something very much

Meanwhile, the Bosnian Muslims **revile** them (peacekeepers) for standing by when women and children are shot.

Word Families: **revilement** *n.;* **reviler** *n.*

6. PURLOIN   [pər'lɔɪn] *v.* to steal something secretly   **rhyming sound -oin**

Everyone is issued a user name and a password so secret that it has to be hidden in a "safe place" lest someone **purloins** it.

7. adjoin   [ə'dʒɔɪn] *v.* to be next to

Canada and Mexico **adjoin** the United States of America.

Word Families: **adjoining** *adj.*

8. conjoin   [kən'dʒɔɪn] *v.* to join two or more things, or become joined

All this will occur because on September 3, Saturn will **conjoin** the Sun.

9. disjoin   [dɪs'dʒɔɪn] *v.* to disconnect parts, things, or ideas

After you **disjoin** the domain, shut down the client computer before you reconnect it to the new domain.

10. rejoin   [ˌri'dʒɔɪn] *v.* to join again

However, by its full compliance, Iraq will gain the opportunity to **rejoin** the international community.

SENTENCE COMPLETION

Choose one of the new words to complete each sentence below. Make changes if necessary.

puerile	agile	docile	exile	futile
purloin	adjoin	conjoin	disjoin	rejoin

1. Circus monkeys are trained to be very _____ and obedient.

2. We waited in an _____ office.

3. Thou shall not _____ the gods, nor curse the ruler of you people.

4. He said that he never heard anything so _____ before.

5. The next big day to watch will be Sunday, March 7, when Mercury will _____ Jupiter.

6. Some countries _____ American technology as it comes off the drawing boards with the help of their governments.

7. Just as physical exercise is essential for a strong body, mental exercise is equally essential for a sharp and _____ mind.

8. Henry has apologized for his bad behavior and should be allowed to _____ the

   group with a clean sheet.

9. It can lift rate of zinc reclamation, _____ the lead and zinc.

10. It is always _____ to try to hold back the progress of history.

DEFINITION MATCHING

Choose one of the new words to match each definition below.

puerile	agile	docile	exile	futile
purloin	adjoin	conjoin	disjoin	rejoin

11. to be next to   _____

12. to join again

    _____

13. to join two or more things, or become joined

    _____

14. to disconnect parts, things, or ideas

    _____

15. to steal something secretly

    _____

16. silly and childish

    _____

17. to hate and criticize someone or something

    _____

18. (of a person or animal) easily controlled

    _____

19. unsuccessful, or useless

    _____

20. able to move quickly and easily

    _____

WRITING SENTENCES

Use each new word in the box to write an original sentence.

puerile	agile	docile	exile	futile
purloin	adjoin	conjoin	disjoin	rejoin

21._____

22._____

23._____

24._____

25._____

26._____

27._____

28._____

29._____

30._____

UNIT 33

MEMORY TIPS:

Word building with Roots, Prefixes, and Suffixes:

---

ify	make, cause; as *putrefy, classify, justify, qualify, sanctify*
inter	between, among; as *interview*
pre	before; as *preview*
re	back, again; as *review*
sanct	holy; as *sanctify*

NEW WORDS

purview	preview	review	worldview	interview
putrefy	classify	justify	qualify	sanctify

1. PURVIEW   ['pɜrvju] *n.* scope or range of activity or outlook   **rhyming sound –iew**

These are questions that lie outside the **purview** of our inquiry.

2. preview   ['pri,vju] *n.* advance showing of a film or exhibition; *v.* to provide a description of something that will happen in the future

You will be able to see a **preview** of the image that you upload.

Word Families: **previews** *n. pl.*

3. review   [rɪ'vju] *n.* critical assessment of a book, film, etc.; *v.* to examine

140

Officials said the investigation does not amount to a full safety **review**.

Word Families: **reviewal** *n.;* **reviewable** *adj.*

4. worldview   ['wɜːldvju:] *n.* the way one sees and understands the world events

Worldview is total knowledge and evaluation of human to the whole world.

5. interview   ['ɪntərˌvju] *adj.* questioning of someone or a famous person; discussion between a job-seeker and employer; *v.* to conduct an interview with

There'll be an **interview** with Mr. Brown after the news.

Word Families: **interviewee** *n.;* **interviewer** *n.*

6. PUTREFY   ['pjutrɪˌfaɪ] *v.* to decay   **rhyming sound –fy, -ify**

Incomplete pre-digestion process causes partially digested proteins to **putrefy** in the intestines forming toxic substances.

7. classify   ['klæsəˌfaɪ] *v.* to divide into groups with similar characteristics; to declare (information) to be officially secret

Rocks can be **classified** according to their mode of origin.

Word Families: **classification** *n.;* **classifiable** *adj.*

8. justify   ['dʒʌstɪˌfaɪ] *v.* to prove right or reasonable

Several reasons were put forward to **justify** the imposition of censorship.

Word Families: **justification** *n.;* **justifier** *n.;* **justificatory** *adj.*

9. qualify   ['kwɑləˌfaɪ] *v.* to provide or be provided with the abilities for a task

To **qualify** for maternity leave, you must have worked for the same employer for at least two years.

Word Families: **qualification** *n;* **qualifier** *n.;* **qualified** *adj.*

10. sanctify   ['sæŋktəˌfaɪ] *v.* to make someone or something holy

I believe that it is one of the special achievements of Grace to **sanctify** the whole of life, riches included.

Word Families: **sanctification** *n.;* **sanctifier** *n.;* **sanctifiable** *adj.*

SENTENCE COMPLETION

Choose one of the new words to complete each sentence below. Make changes if necessary.

purview	preview	review	worldview	interview
putrefy	classify	justify	qualify	sanctify

1. Am I going to allow bitterness to poison and _____ my soul, or am I going to invite God to empower me to let the anger go?

2. The _____ is uncritical of the violence in the film.

3. The police immediately _____ the man's death as a suicide.

4. They attended a sneak _____ of the winter fashion collection.

5. My intellect was on call to expand its _____ and comprehend.

6. They found it hard to _____ their son's lowering his colors.

7. Mental imagery belongs to the _____ of philosophy and cognitive psychology.

8. She is trying to make amends for her marriage not being _____.

9. Our team _____ for the final by beating Vancouver Canucks on Tuesday.

10. The police _____ the driver, but had no evidence to go on.

DEFINITION MATCHING

Choose one of the new words to match each definition below.

purview	preview	review	worldview	interview
putrefy	classify	justify	qualify	sanctify

11. to declare (information) to be officially secret _____

12. to provide or be provided with the abilities for _____

13. the way one sees and understands world events _____

14. to make someone or something holy _____

15. to prove right or reasonable _____

16. advance showing of a film or exhibition _____

17. to decay _____

18. scope or range of activity or outlook _____

19. critical assessment of a book, film, etc. _____

20. questioning of someone or a famous person _____

WRITING SENTENCES

Use each new word in the box to write an original sentence.

purview	preview	review	worldview	interview
putrefy	classify	justify	qualify	sanctify

21._____

22._____

23._____

24._____

25._____

26._____

27._____

28._____

29._____

30._____

UNIT 34

MEMORY TIPS:

Word building with Roots, Prefixes, and Suffixes:

---

ac, as	to; as *acquire, aspire*
con	together; as *conspire*
mar	sea; as *marine*

NEW WORDS

quagmire	acquire	aspire	conspire	respire
quarantine	chlorine	cuisine	marine	pristine

1. QUAGMIRE ['kwæg,maɪr] *n.* soft wet area of land   **rhyming sound –ire**

He who tries to conceal his fault for fear of criticism will sink deeper and deeper in the **quagmire** of errors.

Word Families: **quagmires** *n. pl.*

2. acquire [ə'kwaɪr] *v.* to gain; to get

Should Iraq **acquire** fissile material, it would be able to build a nuclear weapon within a year.

Word Families: **acquisition** *n.;* **acquiree** *n.;* **acquirer** *n.;* **acquirable** *adj.*

3. aspire [ə'spaɪr] *n.* to want to achieve something or to be successful

Literally, he lived only to **aspire** after what was good and great, certainly.

Word Families: **aspiration** *n.*

4. conspire   [kənˈspaɪr] *v.* to plan a crime (something bad) together in secret

The oil companies **conspire** every year to increase the price of oil.

Word Families: **conspiracy** *n.;* **conspirator** *n.;* **conspiratorial** *adj.*

5. respire   [rɪˈspaɪr] *v.* to breathe

He also discovered that plants **respire** in the same way as animals,

taking up oxygen and giving out carbon dioxide.

Word Families: **respiration** *n.;* **respiratory** *adj.*

6. QUARANTINE [ˈkwɔrənˌtin] *n.* a period of enforced seclusion to prevent contagion
rhyming sound -ine

The health officials placed the ship's crew in **quarantine**.

7. chlorine   [ˈklɔrin] *n.* a gas with a strong smell used to kill bacteria in the pool

Her eyes were red and sore because of all the **chlorine** in the pool.

8. cuisine   [kwɪˈzin] *n.* style of cooking

This village has its own traditional dress, **cuisine**, folklore and handicrafts.

Word Families: **cuisine** *n.pl.*

9. marine   [məˈrin] *adj.* living in or happening in the ocean; *n.* a soldier in the marine

corps.

He was one of eighteen researchers who wrote the **Marine** Policy paper.

10. pristine   [ˈprɪˌstin] *adj.* clean, new, and unused

The secret behind the **pristine** complexion of these exotic women was Pearl
Powder.

SENTENCE COMPLETION

Choose one of the new words to complete each sentence below. Make changes if necessary.

quagmire	acquire	aspire	conspire	respire
quarantine	chlorine	cuisine	marine	pristine

1. General Motors _____ a 50% stake in Saab for about $400 million.

2. The dog was kept in _____ for six months.

3. The hotel has a large dining room serving superb local _____.

4. They _____ to be gentlemen, though they fell far short of the ideal.

5. If you think your water has a strong taste of _____, try boiling it.

6. They tried artificial _____ but it was of no avail.

7. The heavy rain had turned the pitch into a _____.

8. Those who plot and _____ will certainly come to no good end.

9. New Zealand is renowned for the _____, natural beauty of its environment

   beyond comparison.

10. Aides to the president say Mr. Bush has protected more of the _____ environment
    than any of his predecessors.

DEFINITION MATCHING

Choose one of the new words to match each definition below.

quagmire	acquire	aspire	conspire	respire
quarantine	chlorine	cuisine	marine	pristine

11. to breathe   _____

12. living in or happening in the ocean   _____

13. soft wet area of land   _____

14. time for enforced seclusion to prevent contagion _____

15. clean, new, and unused _____

16. to want to achieve something or to be successful _____

17. style of cooking _____

18. a gas with a strong smell used to kill bacteria _____

19. to gain; to get _____

20. to plan a crime (bad things) together in secret _____

WRITING SENTENCES

Use each new word in the box to write an original sentence.

quagmire	acquire	aspire	conspire	respire
quarantine	chlorine	cuisine	marine	pristine

21. _____

22. _____

23. _____

24. _____

25. _____

26. _____

27. _____

28. _____

29. _____

30. _____

UNIT 35

MEMORY TIPS:

Word building with Roots, Prefixes, and Suffixes:

---

chron	time; as *chronological*
ence	state of; as *sequence, diligence, indulgence, quintessence, intelligence*
il	not; as *illogical*
in	into, in, on; as *indulgence*

NEW WORDS

quintessence	sequence	diligence	indulgence	intelligence
quizzical	radical	illogical	sabbatical	chronological

1. **QUINTESSENCE** [kwɪnˈtes(ə)ns] *n.* most perfect representation of quality or state

    rhyming sound –ence

    The development and evolution of liberalism show the **quintessence** of the two political traditions from beginning to end.

    Word Families: **quintessential** *adj.*

2. **sequence**   [ˈsikwəns] *n.* the successive order of two or more things

    The book is more satisfying if you read each chapter in **sequence**.

3. **diligence**   [ˈdɪlɪdʒəns] *n.* care and perseverance

Genius is nothing but wit and **diligence**.

Word Families: **diligent** *adj.;* **diligently** *adj.*

4. indulgence [ɪn'dʌldʒəns] *n.* act of doing something that is not good for you

The woman seldom allows herself any moment of **indulgence** in self-pity.

Word Families: **indulgences** *n. pl.*

5. intelligence [ɪn'telɪdʒəns] *n.* quality of being intelligent; secret government or military information

She used her good looks to compensate her lack of **intelligence**.

Families: **intelligent** *adj.*

6. QUIZZICAL ['kwɪzɪkəl] *adj.* questioning and mocking   **rhyming sound -ical**

His face wore a somewhat **quizzical**, almost impertinent air.

Word Families: **quizzicality** *n.;* **quizzically** *adv.*

7. radical ['rædɪk(ə)l] *adj.* advocating drastic reform of existing institutions; *n.* an extreme liberal in politics

The county now needs stability instead of **radical** changes in its policies.

Word Families: **radicalism** *n.;* **radically** *adv.*

8. illogical [ɪ'lɑdʒɪk(ə)l] *adj.* not based on clear facts, reasons, or principles

There are some people who will use any kind of argument, no matter how **illogical**, so long as they can score off an opponent.

Word Families: **illogicality** *n.;* **illogically** *adv.*

9. sabbatical [sə'bætɪk(ə)l] *adj., n.* (denoting) leave for study, rest, or travel

Dr. Samuel Johnson is on **sabbatical** in Europe this year.

Word Families: **sabbaticals** *n.pl.*

10. chronological [ˌkrɑnə'lɑdʒɪk(ə)l] *adj.* arranged or listed in the order of occurrence

The paintings are exhibited in **chronological** sequence.

Word Families: **chronologically** *adv.*

SENTENCE COMPLETION

Choose one of the new words to complete each sentence below. Make changes if necessary.

quintessence	sequence	diligence	indulgence	intelligence
quizzical	radical	illogical	sabbatical	chronological

1. The police are pursuing their inquiries with great _____.

2. He had a _____ expression on his face when he got in.

3. It is clearly _____ to maintain such a proposition.

4. He was the _____ of all that Eva most deeply loathed.

5. There was some sort of _____ psychiatric treatment involved.

6. Jenny Jones spent her _____ writing a novel.

7. The project is nothing less than mapping every gene _____ in the human body.

8. The purpose of _____ is to provide information on how the enemy can be beaten.

9. The car is one of my few _____.

10. The items are arranged in _____ order, with the most recent at the top.

DEFINITION MATCHING

Choose one of the new words to match each definition below.

quintessence	sequence	diligence	indulgence	intelligence
quizzical	radical	illogical	sabbatical	chronological

11. an extreme liberal in politics _____

12. (denoting) leave for study, rest, or travel _____

13. the successive order of two or more things _____

14. arranged or listed in the order of occurrence _____

15. not based on clear facts, reasons, or principles _____

16. act of doing something that is not good for you _____

17. quality of being intelligent _____

18. most perfect of quality or state _____

19. questioning and mocking _____

20. care and perseverance _____

WRITING SENTENCES

Use each new word in the box to write an original sentence.

quintessence	sequence	diligence	indulgence	intelligence
quizzical	radical	illogical	sabbatical	chronological

21._____

22._____

23._____

24._____

25._____

26._____

27._____

28._____

29._____

30._____

ANSWER KEY

UNIT 1

SENTENCE COMPLETION

1. inauspicious 2. rotund 3. laborious 4. jocund 5. rubicund 6. pernicious 7. moribund 8. refund 9. prejudicious 10. avaricious

DEFINITION MATCHING

11. rotund 12. laborious 13. rubicund 14. prejudicious 15. refund 16. pernicious 17. avaricious 18. moribund 19. inauspicious 20. jocund

WRITING SENTENCES

Answers will vary based on students' personal experiences.

UNIT 2

SENTENCE COMPLETION

1. advocates 2. lambent 3. lacerated 4. imminent 5. precipitate 6. nascent 7. intimidate 8. pertinent 9. consolidated 10. penitent

DEFINITION MATCHING

11. precipitate 12. pertinent 13. consolidate 14. penitent 15. intimidate 16. lacerate 17. imminent 18. lambent 19. nascent 20. advocate

WRITING SENTENCES

Answers will vary based on students' personal experiences.

UNIT 3

SENTENCE COMPLETION

1. largess 2. lampoon 3. digress 4. duress 5. monsoon 6. lagoon 7. obsess 8. platoon 9. tycoon 10. transgress

DEFINITION MATCHING

11. digress 12. obsess 13. duress 14. monsoon 15. transgress 16. tycoon 17. largess 18. lagoon 19. platoon 20. lampoon

WRITING SENTENCES

Answers will vary based on students' personal experiences.

UNIT 4

SENTENCE COMPLETION

1. profusion 2.precision 3. conducive 4. legion 5. abortive 6. cumulatively 7. introversion 8. lucrative 9. fusions 10. diminutive

DEFINITION MATCHING

11. abortive 12. lucrative 13. fusion 14. diminutive 15. precision 16. cumulative 17. introversion 18. legion 19. conducive 20. profusion

WRITING SENTENCES

Answers will vary based on students' personal experiences.

UNIT 5

SENTENCE COMPLETION

1. rid 2.dull 3. acrid 4. lurid 5. lull 6. forbid 7. gull 8. skull 9. null 10. rigid

DEFINITION MATCHING

11. lurid 12. null 13. acrid 14. forbid 15. rigid 16. lull 17. skull 18. gull 19. rid 20. dull

WRITING SENTENCES

Answers will vary based on students' personal experiences.

UNIT 6

SENTENCE COMPLETION

1. addiction 2.jurisdiction 3. convictions 4. malediction 5. resign 6. consign 7. malign 8. friction 9. assign 10. align

DEFINITION MATCHING

11. align 12. addiction 13. jurisdiction 14. consign 15. friction 16. conviction 17. resign 18. malign 19. assign 20. malediction

WRITING SENTENCES

Answers will vary based on students' personal experiences.

UNIT 7

SENTENCE COMPLETION

1. morality 2.mercenary 3. fatality 4. materiality 5. centenary 6. formality 7. planetary 8. mortuary 9. brutality 10. adversary

DEFINITION MATCHING

11. mortuary 12. morality 13. planetary 14. fatality 15. centenary 16. materiality 17. mercenary 18. adversary 19. brutality 20. formality

WRITING SENTENCES

Answers will vary based on students' personal experiences.

UNIT 8

SENTENCE COMPLETION

1. oscillate 2.mitigate 3. mollify 4. propagate 5. certify 6. innate 7. rectify 8. ossify 9. vilification 10. emulate

DEFINITION MATCHING

11. vilify 12. rectify 13. ossify 14. innate 15. certify 16. oscillate 17. emulate 18. propagate 19. mollify 20. mitigate

WRITING SENTENCES

Answers will vary based on students' personal experiences.

UNIT 9

SENTENCE COMPLETION

1. penchant 2.mordant 3. morose 4. recalcitrant 5. verbose 6. foreclose 7. petulant 8. dispose 9. compose 10. rampant

DEFINITION MATCHING

11. petulant 12. verbose 13. foreclose 14. recalcitrant 15. dispose 16. mordant 17. morose 18. compose 19. penchant 20. rampant

WRITING SENTENCES

Answers will vary based on students' personal experiences.

UNIT 10

SENTENCE COMPLETION

1. insane 2.humane 3. extent 4. mundane 5. aliment 6. hurricane 7. consented 8. regiment 9. profaned 10. munificent

DEFINITION MATCHING

11. regiment 12. consent 13. aliment 14. profane 15. extent 16. mundane 17. hurricane 18. humane 19. munificent 20. insane

WRITING SENTENCES

Answers will vary based on students' personal experiences.

UNIT 11

SENTENCE COMPLETION

1. precarious 2. tererarious 3. multifarious 4. vicarious 5. mimesis 6. nefarious 7. nemesis 8. thesis 9. telekinesis 10. exegesis

DEFINITION MATCHING

11. telekinesis 12. multifarious 13. precarious 14. exegesis 15. mimesis 16. nefarious 17. thesis 18. tererarious 19. nemesis 20. vicarious

WRITING SENTENCES

Answers will vary based on students' personal experiences.

UNIT 12

SENTENCE COMPLETION

1. atmospheric 2.troglodyte 3. esoteric 4. neoteric 5. neophyte 6. byte 7. acolyte 8. proselytes 9. generic 10. numeric

DEFINITION MATCHING

11. troglodyte 12. esoteric 13. acolyte 14. neoteric 15. neophyte 16. atmospheric 17. numeric 18. byte 19. generic 20. proselyte

WRITING SENTENCES

Answers will vary based on students' personal experiences.

UNIT 13

SENTENCE COMPLETION

1. fettle 2.nettle 3. discard 4. niggard 5. retard 6. settled 7. safeguards 8. mettle 9. bard 10. unsettle

DEFINITION MATCHING

11. retard 12. settle 13. safeguard 14. unsettle 15. discard 16. nettle 17. bard 18. niggard 19. mettle 20. fettle

WRITING SENTENCES

Answers will vary based on students' personal experiences.

UNIT 14

SENTENCE COMPLETION

1. nutritious 2.precious 3. obnoxious 4. noxious 5. signatory 6. purgatory 7. nugatory 8. defamatory 9. ostentatious 10. mandatory

DEFINITION MATCHING

11. obnoxious 12. purgatory 13. nutritious 14. signatory 15. mandatory 16. noxious 17. defamatory 18. ostentatious 19. nugatory 20. precious

WRITING SENTENCES

Answers will vary based on students' personal experiences.

UNIT 15

SENTENCE COMPLETION

1. renaissance 2.nuance 3. castigate 4. obeisance 5. articulate 6. enhance 7. inveterate 8. askance 9. obfuscate 10. deprecate

DEFINITION MATCHING

11. castigate 12. deprecate 13. enhance 14. articulate 15. inveterate 16. obeisance 17. obfuscate 18. nuance 19. renaissance 20. askance

WRITING SENTENCES

Answers will vary based on students' personal experiences.

UNIT 16

SENTENCE COMPLETION

1. extrapolate 2.deludes 3. obtrude 4. enunciate 5. aptitudes 6. rectitude 7. exculpated 8. lassitude 9. objurgate 10. facilitate

DEFINITION MATCHING

11. aptitude 12. rectitude 13. lassitude 14. extrapolate 15. delude 16. objurgate 17. facilitate 18. exculpate 19. obtrude 20. enunciate

WRITING SENTENCES

Answers will vary based on students' personal experiences.

UNIT 17

SENTENCE COMPLETION

1. fractious 2.hierarchy 3. oligarchy 4. odious 5. patriarchy 6. anarchy 7. facetious 8. monarchy 9. disputatious 10. fortuitous

DEFINITION MATCHING

11. anarchy 12. hierarchy 13. facetious 14. fortuitous 15. patriarchy 16. odious 17. oligarchy 18. monarchy 19. fractious 20. disputatious

WRITING SENTENCES

Answers will vary based on students' personal experiences.

UNIT 18

SENTENCE COMPLETION

1. adolescent 2.fervent 3. captious 4. horrendous 5. opalescence 6. putrescent 7. lecherous 8. opprobrious 9. ferment 10. mellifluous

DEFINITION MATCHING

11. lecherous 12. mellifluous 13. ferment 14. horrendous 15. opprobrious 16. opalescent 17. captious 18. fervent 19. adolescent 20. putrescent

WRITING SENTENCES

Answers will vary based on students' personal experiences.

UNIT 19

SENTENCE COMPLETION

1. clone 2.inculcate 3. condone 4. immaculately 5. cyclone 6. instigate 7. ozone 8. originate 9. silicone 10. litigate

DEFINITION MATCHING

11. immaculate 12. cyclone 13. inculcate 14. silicone 15. condone 16. originate 17. clone 18. litigate 19. ozone 20. instigate

WRITING SENTENCES

Answers will vary based on students' personal experiences.

UNIT 20

SENTENCE COMPLETION

1. tractable 2. Equinox 3. palpable 4. smallpox 5. orthodox 6. jukebox 7. immutable 8. irreparable 9. paradox 10. viable

DEFINITION MATCHING

11. equinox 12. orthodox 13. tractable 14. smallpox 15. jukebox 16. palpable 17. paradox 18. irreparable 19. viable 20. immutable

WRITING SENTENCES

Answers will vary based on students' personal experiences.

UNIT 21

SENTENCE COMPLETION

1. disparity 2.amorphous 3. brevity 4. alacrity 5. arduous 6. depravity 7. parity

8. anonymous 9. ambiguous 10. parsimonious

DEFINITION MATCHING

11. ambiguous 12. anonymous 13. arduous 14. alacrity 15. amorphous 16. parity 17. parsimonious 18. depravity 19. brevity 20. disparity

WRITING SENTENCES

Answers will vary based on students' personal experiences.

UNIT 22

SENTENCE COMPLETION

1. impunity 2.paucity 3. jury 4. fury 5. humility 6. penury 7. probity 8. perjury 9. frugality 10. Mercury

DEFINITION MATCHING

11. impunity 12. mercury 13. probity 14. jury 15. perjury 16. penury 17. paucity 18. fury 19. frugality 20. humility

WRITING SENTENCES

Answers will vary based on students' personal experiences.

UNIT 23

SENTENCE COMPLETION

1. abnegation 2.implication 3. allegory 4. perdition 5. peremptory 6. adulation 7. dilatory 8. aspersion 9. perfunctory 10. Inventory

DEFINITION MATCHING

11. implication 12. inventory 13. allegory 14. perfunctory 15. perdition 16.

peremptory 17. dilatory 18. abnegation 19. adulation 20. aspersion

WRITING SENTENCES

Answers will vary based on students' personal experiences.

UNIT 24

SENTENCE COMPLETION

1. momentous 2.vociferous 3. tenuous 4. peruse 5. perfidious 6. ominously 7. fuse 8. abused 9. interfusion 10. muse

DEFINITION MATCHING

11. muse 12. interfuse 13. perfidious 14. abuse 15. fuse 16. tenuous 17. vociferous 18. peruse 19. ominous 20. momentous

WRITING SENTENCES

Answers will vary based on students' personal experiences.

UNIT 25

SENTENCE COMPLETION

1. evasiveness 2.dissuasive 3. persuasive 4. pervasive 5. intuition 6. coalition 7. rendition 8. acquisition 9. abrasive 10. petition

DEFINITION MATCHING

11. petition 12. rendition 13. abrasive 14. acquisition 15. intuition 16. persuasive 17. dissuasive 18. coalition 19. evasive 20. pervasive

WRITING SENTENCES

Answers will vary based on students' personal experiences.

UNIT 26

SENTENCE COMPLETION

1. systemic 2.endemic 3. epistemic 4. polemic 5. portend 6. blend 7. epidemic 8. reprehended 9. apprehend 10. amend

DEFINITION MATCHING

11. apprehend 12. reprehend 13. polemic 14. amend 15. blend 16. endemic 17. portend 18. epidemic 19. epistemic 20. systemic

WRITING SENTENCES

Answers will vary based on students' personal experiences.

UNIT 27

SENTENCE COMPLETION

1. spaciousness 2. specious 3. inception 4. atrocious 5. concept 6. intercepted 7. precept 8. inept 9. ferocious 10. precocious

DEFINITION MATCHING

11. precocious 12. specious 13. precept 14. intercept 15. ferocious 16. concept 17. atrocious 18. spacious 19. incept 20. inept

WRITING SENTENCES

Answers will vary based on students' personal experiences.

UNIT 28

SENTENCE COMPLETION

1. profligate 2. repudiate 3. elaborate 4. preponderate 5. prerogative 6. prate 7. preservative 8. derivative 9. figurative 10. correlative

DEFINITION MATCHING

11. profligate 12. prerogative 13. preponderate 14. preservative 15. figurative 16. prate 17. derivative 18. repudiate 19. correlative 20. elaborate

WRITING SENTENCES

Answers will vary based on students' personal experiences.

UNIT 29

SENTENCE COMPLETION

1. scoliosis 2. prolific 3. prognosis 4. specific 5. horrific 6. Diagnosis 7. terrific 8. colorific 9. hypnosis 10. Tuberculosis

DEFINITION MATCHING

11. tuberculosis 12. horrific 13. colorific 14. scoliosis 15. terrific 16. hypnosis 17. specific 18. diagnosis 19. prolific 20. prognosis

WRITING SENTENCES

Answers will vary based on students' personal experiences.

UNIT 30

SENTENCE COMPLETION

1. relegate 2. deviated 3. eradication 4. prognosticate 5. differentiate 6. initiated 7. implicate 8. propitiate 9. mediate 10. reiterate

DEFINITION MATCHING

11. eradicate 12. differentiate 13. propitiate 14. mediate 15. initiate 16. prognosticate 17. reiterate 18. deviate 19. implicate 20. relegate

WRITING SENTENCES

Answers will vary based on students' personal experiences.

UNIT 31

SENTENCE COMPLETION

1. cholesterol 2. diffident 3. evident 4. alcohol 5. protocol 6. incident 7. provident 8. menthol 9. coincident 10. parasol

DEFINITION MATCHING

11. coincident 12. parasol 13. cholesterol 14. incident 15. evident 16. protocol 17. provident 18. diffident 19. menthol 20. alcohol

WRITING SENTENCES

Answers will vary based on students' personal experiences.

UNIT 32

SENTENCE COMPLETION

1. docile 2. adjoining 3. revile 4. puerile 5. conjoin 6. purloin 7. agile 8. rejoin

9. disjoin 10. futile

DEFINITION MATCHING

11. adjoining 12. rejoin 13. conjoin 14. disjoin 15. purloin 16. puerile 17. revile 18. docile 19. futile 20. agile

WRITING SENTENCES

Answers will vary based on students' personal experiences.

UNIT 33

SENTENCE COMPLETION

1. putrefy 2. review 3. classified 4. preview 5. worldview 6. justify 7. purview 8. sanctified 9. qualified 10. interviewed

DEFINITION MATCHING

11. classify 12. qualify 13. worldview 14. sanctify 15. justify 16. preview 17. putrefy 18. purview 19. review 20. interview

WRITING SENTENCES

Answers will vary based on students' personal experiences.

UNIT 34

SENTENCE COMPLETION

1. acquired 2. quarantine 3. cuisine 4. aspired 5. chlorine 6. respiration 7. quagmire 8. conspire 9. pristine 10. marine

DEFINITION MATCHING

11. respire 12. marine 13. quagmire 14.

quarantine 15. pristine 16. aspire 17. cuisine 18. chlorine 19. acquire 20. conspire

WRITING SENTENCES

Answers will vary based on students' personal experiences.

UNIT 35

SENTENCE COMPLETION

1. diligence 2. quizzical 3. illogical 4. quintessence 5. radical 6. sabbatical 7. sequence 8. intelligence 9. indulgences 10. chronological

DEFINITION MATCHING

11. radical 12. sabbatical 13. sequence 14. chronological 15. illogical 16. indulgence 17. intelligence 18. quintessence 19. quizzical 20. diligence

WRITING SENTENCES

Answers will vary based on students' personal experiences.

WORD INDEX

This index lists 350 absolutely essential IELTS key words appeared in this book. You may use the list as a dictionary to find out the definitions, samples sentences, and the uses of each word to boost your retention.

A

Abnegation 99

Abortive 23

Abrasive 107

Abuse 103

Acolyte 55

Acquisition 107

Acrid 27

Addiction 31

Adjoin 135

Adolescent 79

Adulation 99

Adversary 35

Advocate 15

Agile 135

Alacrity 91

Alcohol 131

Align 31

Aliment 47

Allegory 99

Ambiguous 91

Amend 111

Amorphous 91

Anarchy 75

Anonymous 91

Apprehend 111

Aptitude 71

Acquire 143

Arduous 91

Articulate 67

Askance 67

Aspersion 99

Aspire 143

Assign 31

Atmospheric 55

Atrocious 115

Avaricious 11

B

Bard 59

Blend 111

Brevity 91

Brutality 35

Byte 55

C

Captious 79

Castigate 67

Centenary 35

Certify 39

Chlorine 143

Cholesterol 131

Chronological 147

Classify 139

Clone 83

Coalition 107

Coincident 131

Colorific 123

Compose 43

Concept 115

Condone 83

Conducive 23

Conjoin 135

Consent 47

Consign 31

Consolidate 15

Conspire 143

Conviction 31

Correlative 119

Cuisine 143

Cumulative 23

Cyclone 83

D

Defamatory 63

Delude 71

Depravity 91

Deprecate 67

Derivative 119

Deviate 127

Diagnosis 123

Differentiate 127

Diffident 131

Digress 19

Dilatory 99

Diligence 147

Diminutive 23

Discard 59

Disjoin 135

Disparity 91

Dispose 43

Disputatious 75

Dissuasive 107

Docile 135

Dull 27

Duress 19

Esoteric 55

Evasive 107

Evident 131

Exculpate 71

Exegesis 51

Exile 135

Extent 47

Extrapolate 71

E

Elaborate 119

Emulate 39

Enunciate 71

Endemic 111

Enhance 67

Epidemic 111

Epistemic 111

Equinox 87

Eradicate 127

F

Facetious 75

Facilitate 71

Factious 75

Fatality 35

Ferment 79

Ferocious 115

Fervent 79

Fettle 59

Figurative 119

Forbid 27

Foreclose 43

Formality 35

Fortuitous 75

Friction 31

Frugality 95

Fury 95

Fuse 103

Fusion 23

Futile 135

G

Generic 55

Gull 27

H

Hierarchy 75

Horrendous 79

Horrific 123

Humane 47

Humility 95

Hurricane 47

Hypnosis 123

I

Illogical 147

Immaculate 83

Imminent 15

Immutable 87

Implicate 127

Implication 99

Impunity 95

Inauspicious 11

Incept 115

Incident 131

Inculcate 83

Indulgence 147

Inept 115

Initiate 127

Innate 39

Insane 47

Instigate 83

Intelligence 147

Intercept 115

Interfuse 103

Interview 139

Intimidate 15

Introversion 23

Intuition 107

Inventory 99

Inveterate 67

Irreparable 87

J

Jocund 11

Jukebox 87

Jurisdiction 31

Jury 95

Justify 139

L

Laborious 11

Lacerate 15

Lambent 15

Lagoon 19

Lampoon 19

Largess 19

Lassitude 71

Lecherous 79

Legion 23

Litigate 83

Lucrative 23

Lull 27

Lurid 27

M

Malediction 31

Malign 31

Mandatory 63

Marine 143

Materiality 35

Mediate 127

Mellifluous 79

Mimesis 51

Menthol 131

Mercenary 35

Mercury 95

Mettle 59

Mitigate 39

Mollify 39

Momentous 103

Monarchy 75

Monsoon 19

Morality 35

Mordant 43

Moribund 11

Morose 43

Mortuary 35

Multifarious 51

Mundane 47

Munificent 47

Muse 103

N

Nascent 15

Nefarious 51

Nemesis 51

Neophyte 55

Neoteric 55

Nettle 59

Niggard 59

Noxious 63

Nuance 67

Nugatory 63

Null 27

Numeric 55

Nutritious 63

O

Obeisance 67

Obfuscate 67

Objurgate 71

Obsess 19

Obtrude 71

Odious 75

Oligarchy 75

Ominous 103

Opalescent 79

Opprobrious 79

Originate 83

Orthodox 87

Oscillate 39

Ossify 39

Ostentatious 63

Ozone 83

P

Palpable 87

Paradox 87

Parasol 131

Parity 91

Parsimonious 91

Patriarchy 75

Paucity 95

Penchant 43

Penitent 15

Penury 95

Perdition 99

Peremptory 99

Perfidious 103

Perfunctory 99

Perjury 95

Pernicious 11

Persuasive 107

Pertinent 15

Peruse 103

Pervasive 107

Petition 107

Petulant 43

Planetary 35

Platoon 19

Polemic 111

Portend 111

Prate 119

Precarious 51

Precept 115

Precious 63

Precipitate 15

Precision 23

Precocious 115

Prejudicious 11

Preponderate 119

Prerogative 119

Preservative 119

Preview 139

Pristine 143

Probity 95

Profane 47

Profligate 119

Profusion 23

Prognosis 123

Prognosticate 127

Prolific 123

Propagate 39

Propitiate 127

Proselyte 55

Protocol 131

Provident 131

Puerile 135

Purgatory 63

Purloin 135

Purview 139

Putrefy 139

Putrescent 79

Q

Quagmire 143

Qualify 139

Quarantine 143

Quintessence 147

Quizzical 147

R

Radical 147

Rampant 43

Recalcitrant 43

Rectify 39

Rectitude 71

Refund 11

Regiment 47

Reiterate 127

Rejoin 135

Relegate 127

Renaissance 67

Rendition 107

Reprehend 111

Repudiate 119

Resign 31

Respire 143

Retard 59

Review 139

Rid 27

Rigid 27

Rotund 11

Rubicund 11

S

Sabbatical 147

Safeguard 59

Sanctify 139

Scoliosis 123

Sequence 147

Settle 59

Signatory 63

Silicone 83

Skull 27

Smallpox 87

Spacious 115

Specific 123

Specious 115

Systemic 111

T

Telekinesis 51

Temerarious 51

Tenuous 103

Terrific 123

Thesis 51

Tractable 87

Transgress 19

Troglodyte 55

Tuberculosis 123

Tycoon 19

U

Unsettle 59

V

Verbose 43

Viable 87

Vicarious 51

Vilify 39

Vociferous 103

W

Worldview 139

ACKNOWLEDGMENTS

The author would like to thank his colleagues and students for their invaluable assistance in bringing this book to life.

The author and publisher are grateful to those who have made this publication possible by providing all kinds of support from editing, graphic design, and proof-reading. Efforts have been made to identify the source of materials used in this book, however, it has not always been possible to identify the sources of all the materials used, or to trace the copyright holders. If any omissions are brought to our attention, we will be happy to include the appropriate acknowledgments on reprinting.

ABOUT THE AUTHOR

Dr. Richard Lee is a professor of English and distinguished publishing scholar with numerous books published under his name. His books are available on Amazon, other online stores, and in bookstores worldwide. He pursued his doctoral education at the University of Rochester in New York and the University of British Columbia and received his Ph.D. in English.

CPSIA information can be obtained at www.ICGtesting.com
Printed in the USA
LVOW02s0108161214

419023LV00002B/15/P